Peter Malin

Series Editor: Mari

The White Devil

John Webster

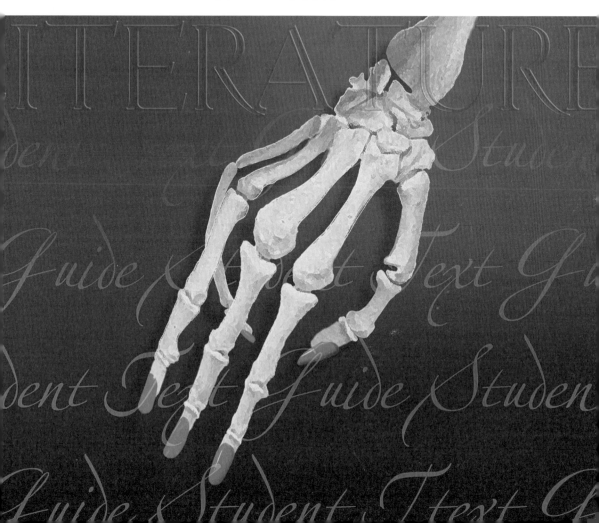

Philip Allan Updates, an imprint of Hodder Education, part of Hachette Livre UK, Market Place, Deddington, Oxfordshire OX15 0SE

Orders
Bookpoint Ltd, 130 Milton Park, Abingdon, Oxfordshire, OX14 4SB
tel: 01235 827720
fax: 01235 400454
e-mail: uk.orders@bookpoint.co.uk
Lines are open 9.00 a.m.–5.00 p.m., Monday to Saturday, with a 24-hour message answering service. You can also order through the Philip Allan Updates website: www.philipallan.co.uk

© Philip Allan Updates 2008

ISBN 978-0-340-97117-8

Impression number 5 4 3 2 1
Year 2012 2011 2010 2009 2008

Printed in Malta

Environmental information
Hachette Livre UK's policy is to use papers that are natural, renewable and recyclable products and made from wood grown in sustainable forests. The logging and manufacturing processes are expected to conform to the environmental regulations of the country of origin.

P01264

Contents

Introduction

Note: the information given in this introductory section relates to the revised specifications in operation from 2009 (AS) and 2010 (A2).

Aims of the guide

The purpose of this Student Text Guide to *The White Devil* is to support your study of the play, whether you are approaching it as an examination text or for coursework. It is not a substitute for your own reading, rereading, thinking and note-making about the text. The ideas about the play contained in this guide are based on the interpretation of one reader. What the examiners want is *your own* considered response, and they can easily recognise an answer that simply repeats a critical viewpoint at second hand. As you use this guide, you should be constantly questioning what it says; you may find yourself disagreeing with some of the analysis, which in itself could form an interesting starting-point for your own interpretative view.

You may well be studying the play as part of a comparative task, either for coursework or examination. This Student Text Guide cannot possibly cover all the other texts with which you might compare it, but focuses only on *The White Devil*. Connections are often made with other texts, however, particularly with plays by Shakespeare and by other dramatists of Webster's period. You can follow up these links for yourself as appropriate; you will find that many of the texts mentioned are covered by other Student Text Guides in this series.

Quotations and line references in this guide refer to the Revels Student Edition of the play, edited by John Russell Brown (1996). If you are using another edition, the references should be easy enough to find, though there may be occasional slight differences, particularly in scenes containing prose.

The remainder of this *Introduction* outlines the principal exam board Assessment Objectives, and offers advice on revision and how to approach both coursework and exam essays. I am indebted to the series editor, Marian Cox, whose own Student Text Guides I have used in composing this introductory section.

The *Text Guidance* section consists of a series of chapters covering key aspects of the play. These include contexts; a scene-by-scene commentary on the play; analysis of characters, language and themes; the play's critical and theatrical afterlife; and a selected glossary of literary terms.

The final section, *Questions and Answers*, includes suggested essay questions, sample essay plans with marking guidelines, and two exemplar essays.

Exam board specifications

It is possible to study *The White Devil* on a number of different specifications, either as a coursework or an examination text. Sometimes you may be asked to write about the play individually, sometimes in comparison with other texts. It is absolutely vital that you scrutinise the specification you are following, so that you know exactly what is required. Your teacher should have all the relevant information, from which you will need to attend to such issues as:

- where *The White Devil* fits into the overall structure of the AS and/or A2 course
- whether you are required to study it alone or in comparison with other texts
- the precise demands of any coursework essays you are required to produce
- the length and format of exam papers and whether you are allowed to have your copy of the text in the exam room with you
- the balance and weighting of the Assessment Objectives tested through your response to *The White Devil*

Assessment Objectives

The revised Assessment Objectives (AOs) for AS and A2 English Literature are common to all boards:

AO1	articulate creative, informed and relevant responses to literary texts, using appropriate terminology and concepts, and coherent, accurate written expression
AO2	demonstrate detailed critical understanding in analysing the ways in which structure, form and language shape meanings in literary texts
AO3	explore connections and comparisons between different literary texts, informed by interpretations of other readers
AO4	demonstrate understanding of the significance and influence of the contexts in which literary texts are written and received

It is essential that you pay close attention to the AOs and their weightings for the board for which you are entered. For example, in AQA Specification B (A2 Unit 3) the AOs are equally weighted; whereas for OCR (A2 Unit 3) the dominant objective is AO3, since the examination demands a *comparative* essay.

Once you have identified the relevant AOs and their weightings, you must address them *explicitly* in your answer, in addition to showing your overall familiarity with and understanding of the text and demonstrating your ability to offer a clear, relevant and convincing argument.

Examinations

The White Devil features as an exam text on two of the revised specifications, and you could be required to write about it individually or in comparison with another text.

Revision advice

For the examined units it is possible that extensive revision will be necessary because the original study of the text took place some time previously. There are no short-cuts to effective exam revision; the only way to know a text well is to have done the necessary studying. If you use the following method you will not only revisit and reassess all your previous work on the text in a manageable way but will be able to distil, organise and retain your knowledge.

If you are revising for a *comparative essay* in the exam, revise the text(s) you are likely to be comparing with *The White Devil* in tandem with it through all of the stages outlined below. Creating a comparative chart would be a useful way of approaching this; it would need to be much larger than the following example:

	The White Devil	(Text 2)	(Text 3)
Themes			
Characters			
Genre			
Cultural context			
Language features			

NB The precise format of the chart would depend on the exact nature of Texts 2/3. A comparison with *Macbeth*, for example, would require a different focus from one with, say, *Wuthering Heights* or Blake's *Songs of Innocence and Experience*.

(**1**) Between a month and a fortnight before the exam, depending on your schedule (a simple list of stages with dates displayed in your room, not a work of art), you will need to reread the text, this time taking stock of all the underlinings and marginal annotations as well. As you read, collect onto sheets of A4 the essential ideas and quotations as you come across them. The acts of selecting key material and recording it as notes are natural ways of stimulating thoughts and aiding memory.

(**2**) Reread the highlighted areas and marginal annotations in your critical extracts and background handouts, and add anything useful from them to your list of notes and quotations. Then reread your previous essays and the teachers' comments.

Selecting what is important is a good way to crytallise your knowledge and understanding.

(3) During the run-up to the exam you need to do lots of practice essay plans to help you identify any gaps in your knowledge and give you practice in planning in 5–8 minutes. A range of titles for you to plan is provided in this guide, some of which can be done as full timed essays. If you have not seen a copy of a real exam paper before you take your first module, ask to see a past paper so that you are familiar with the layout and rubric.

(4) About a week before the exam, reduce your two or three sides of A4 notes to a double-sided postcard of very small dense writing. Collect a group of key words by once again selecting and condensing, and use abbreviations for quotations (first and last word), and character and place names (initials). The act of choosing and writing out the short quotations will help you focus on the essential issues, and to recall them quickly in the exam. Make sure that your selection covers the main themes and includes examples of symbolism, style, comments on character, examples of irony, point of view or other significant aspects of the text.

(5) You now have in a compact, accessible form all the material for any possible essay title. For the few days before the exam, you can read through your handy postcard whenever and wherever you get the opportunity. Each time you read it, which will only take a few minutes, you will be reminding yourself of all the information you will be able to recall in the exam to adapt to the general title or to support an analysis of particular passages.

(6) A fresh, active mind works wonders, and information needs time to settle, so don't try to cram just before the exam. Relax the night before and get a good night's sleep. In this way you will be able to enter the exam room feeling the confidence of the well-prepared candidate.

Approaching an exam essay

Your precise approach to writing an essay in exam conditions will depend on how long you have to write it, the Assessment Objectives that are being tested, and whether you are allowed to have your copy of the text with you in the exam.

Choosing a question

- Choose carefully from any options available.
- The apparently 'easier' choice will not necessarily show you at your best: you might be tempted just to reproduce stale ideas without much thought.
- A question that looks more challenging may well result in much greater engagement with the issues and argument as you write.
- However, you must choose a question that you can approach with confidence.

Planning

- Identify and highlight the key words in the question. As you write the essay, keep checking back to ensure that you are dealing with these.
- If the question requires you to focus on a particular passage, read through it, making brief annotations as you do so. You should know the text well enough not to be baffled by anything the set section contains.
- Brainstorm your ideas on your answer sheet. This should take no more than 3 or 4 minutes. For a comparative essay, your brainstorming could usefully be done on a simplified version of the chart printed in the *Revision advice* section (p. 4), limited to the key focus of the question.
- Plan your essay. You will not have time to create a formal and detailed plan, but you should at least highlight on your brainstormed notes a rational order in which to deal with the points you have identified.
- If the question is in parts, either implicitly or explicitly, make sure you give equal attention to each separate requirement.

Writing

- Write your introductory paragraph. This might briefly set the context, define the question's key words, and give some indication of your line of approach. Sometimes, though, it is better to plunge straight into your analysis without any introductory waffling.
- Keep your mind partly on the quality of your own writing: think about sentence structures, paragraphing, vocabulary choices and use of appropriate technical terms. Remember those words and phrases for moving on to a new point or changing direction: 'However', 'On the other hand', 'Alternatively,' 'Nevertheless', 'Even so', 'In addition' etc. These can be useful paragraph starters.
- Write the rest of the essay. Keep checking back to the key words and cross off each point on your notes/plan as you have dealt with it. Check the time at regular intervals.
- Incorporate short, relevant quotations into your argument, weaving them into the grammatical structure of your own sentences. Make the point of longer quotations clear — don't expect them to speak for themselves.
- Create a brief concluding paragraph that gives an overview of your argument without simply repeating or summarising the points you have made. Your conclusion should sound conclusive even if it does not strongly support a particular interpretation.
- Check through what you have written, looking at both content and accuracy, and make neat corrections where necessary. You may wish to add brief points, using omission marks or asterisks, but don't be tempted to make any major changes.
- Cross out your notes and planning with a neat diagonal line.

Further points

The exam paper is designed to test your ability to structure an argument around the specific issues in a question. You must not simply use the question as a peg on which to hang an essay you are determined to write. If a question or title crops up that you have tackled before, don't just regurgitate your previous essay, but try to think about the issues from a fresh perspective.

Essay questions are usually open ended. Don't assume that you are expected to find a 'right answer'; instead, you need to demonstrate the ability to look at the issue from various angles, and perhaps to reach a qualified conclusion. If you do have strong views of your own, and can argue them convincingly, this is evidence of an informed personal response, but you still need to show an awareness of alternative interpretations. You will learn a great deal about what the examiners are looking for by studying:

- the published details of the subject specification
- the Assessment Objectives being tested in each particular part of the exam
- past exam papers
- the examiners' reports on the previous year's exams

Ask your teacher to go through the relevant parts of these documents with you.

Coursework

You may be studying *The White Devil* as a coursework text on one of a number of specifications, and your coursework essay could be critical, creative or comparative. It is vital that the topic you choose for coursework meets all the relevant Assessment Objectives. For a comparative essay, you need to choose a text that has obvious points of comparison and contrast, for example another Renaissance tragedy, such as *Antony and Cleopatra*, *King Lear* or *The Revenger's Tragedy*, or a text that might be regarded as similarly 'Gothic' in tone, such as *Dracula*, *The Castle of Otranto* or the poems and stories of Edgar Allan Poe; or a text that focuses on cruelty and violence, such as Edward Bond's *Lear* or Ian McEwan's *The Comfort of Strangers*. Wide reading is essential before you make your final choice.

If you are tackling a creative piece for coursework, the exam board will provide considerable guidance on suitable topics and approaches. Make sure you study this before committing yourself to a particular idea.

Although handwritten essays may be permissible, it is far better to word-process your coursework. Not only will this facilitate your own process of composition and redrafting, but it also shows consideration for teachers and moderators who have a large number of lengthy essays to read and assess. Double line spacing and wide margins will help them to annotate your work.

From the moment you begin planning your essay, you need to be aware of how long it is expected to be. Essays that diverge radically from the word limit, in either direction, are penalised. The Edexcel specification is particularly draconian about this, stating that: 'Students are required to include a cumulative word count at the bottom of each page. Teacher-assessors and moderators will discontinue marking once the prescribed word limit is reached'. All computer programs have a word-counting facility that enables you to keep a regular check on the number of words you have written.

Approaching a coursework essay

You should be given a reasonable period of time to produce your essay. Don't assume that this means you can relax. If you have 3 weeks to complete your essay, don't leave it until the middle of the third week before you begin. After all, if you were writing a 45-minute exam essay, you would not sit doing nothing for the first 35 minutes. There are a number of key stages in the coursework writing process:

- Choose your title and discuss it with your teacher as soon as possible.
- Make sure you know what the examiners expect from a coursework essay for the specification you are following. Always focus on the Assessment Objectives that are actually being tested through the coursework unit — ask your teacher to make sure.
- Reread the play (plus any comparative texts to be covered in your essay), as well as all relevant notes and essays you have previously produced. Identify what is relevant and start to allow ideas to develop in your mind.
- Set aside an hour to jot down ideas for the essay and convert them into an essay plan. Share this plan with your teacher and make use of any feedback offered.
- Give yourself a reasonable period to draft the essay, working with your text, your notes and other useful materials around you.
- Keep referring back to the title or question, and make sure that you remain focused on it.
- Allow time for your teacher to read and comment on at least part of your draft.
- Redraft your essay until you are satisfied with it. Keep checking that you have focused on the relevant Assessment Objectives.
- Leave plenty of time to complete your final version. Don't just copy it up from your draft — be prepared to add and edit, rephrase and polish.
- A bibliography will add to the professionalism of your essay. This should list all the texts you have quoted from and consulted. Check with your teacher whether you are required to use any particular format for a bibliography, and do not deviate from it.
- Proofread your essay carefully before handing it in.

Text Guidance

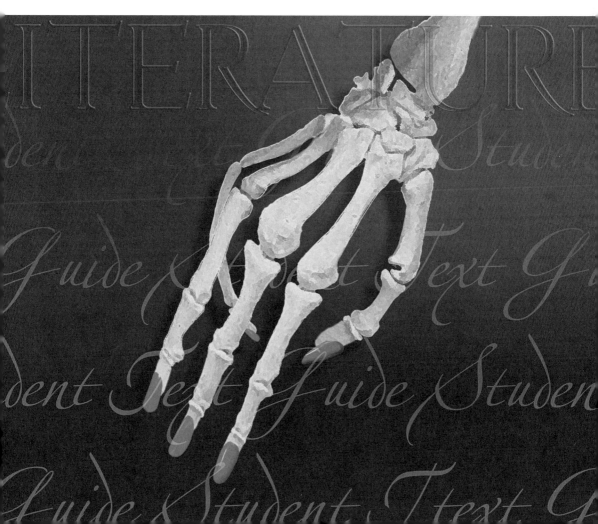

Contexts

Historical and cultural context

The world of the play: a double vision

Ostensibly, the narrative of *The White Devil* is located precisely in time and place. The historical events on which the play is based took place between 1558, when the Duke of Bracciano married Isabella de Medici, and 1585/86, when he died and his second wife Vittoria was murdered. Webster takes great care to create a plausible Renaissance Italian setting. Most of the action takes place in Rome, the centre of both political and religious power. The power struggles of the subsidiary Italian dukedoms are convincingly portrayed, and a web of geographical verisimilitude is cast over the play by its wide range of references to particular places, from other Italian cities such as Florence, Padua and Naples to European countries such as those represented by the foreign ambassadors. Local colour is provided by references to the threat to the coastal regions posed by pirates such as the banished Lodovico; and, more spectacularly, by the authentic representation of a papal election, with all its ceremony and ritual.

However, Webster provides his audience with a distinct double vision of the world of the play. Audiences of the time were used to seeing parallels between their own society and those presented in the theatre, however distant in space and time they may have seemed. Ancient Rome, medieval England or contemporary Europe were all viewed partly for the light they cast on Elizabethan and Jacobean affairs, and Webster ensures, through a range of specific references, that in this play we are never very far from familiar features of London and provincial life. He refers to the very English sport of bowls (I.2.63–65), as well as to features of the English weather such as a so-called Michaelmas spring, or what we might call an Indian summer (V.1.218). More precisely, he mentions the furnace at the 'glass-house', presumably referring to the glass factory in Blackfriars (I.2.138); the 'curtal' horse exhibited by the travelling showman known as Mr Banks in the 1590s (II.2.14); the famous Elizabethan glutton, Wolner, who ate everything from raw meat and fish to iron, glass and oyster-shells (III.3.51); the attempt on Queen Elizabeth's life by poisoning the pommel of her saddle, for which Edward Squire was hanged in 1598 (V.1.70); the 'Artillery Yard' in Bishopsgate where citizens were allowed to practise their military skills (V.6.160); and the lions kept in the zoo at the Tower of London (V.6.266). From such passing references, it is not a huge step to viewing the power struggles of the play, steeped in political, moral and religious hypocrisy, as a reflection of the corruption that was rife among the rich and powerful at the court of James I. In a way, playwrights like Webster were protecting themselves from political censure and censorship by distancing their social criticism through the device of a foreign or historical setting.

The Jacobean world

Politics and society

The hierarchical structure of Elizabethan England was maintained during the reign of James I, who had succeeded Elizabeth in 1603. The power of the monarch, supported by the aristocracy, was increasingly questioned by both the rising middle classes and the economically disadvantaged. The notable extravagance of the court was particularly controversial. The ruling elite promoted and maintained the status quo through a variety of techniques from rigorous control of free speech to the employment of extensive networks of spies — 'intelligencers', to use the word favoured by Webster in the play. Political expediency was encouraged by the ideas of the Italian Niccolò Machiavelli, expounded in *The Prince* (1532), which were selectively interpreted in England as justifying the use of unethical means to acquire and maintain power. The machiavel became a dramatic stereotype, and audiences delighted in the devious machinations of overreaching villains who backed up their schemes with cruelty, torture and murder. Monticelso and Francisco are the most obviously machiavellian characters in the play, but we also see Vittoria manipulating Bracciano into murdering their respective spouses through her account of her supposed dream; Flamineo playing off characters against each other with supreme skill; and Bracciano engaged in hypocritical displays of friendship to achieve his own purposes.

Social mobility was a threat to the established order, too. People were expected to know their place and remain there; to do otherwise was supposedly to risk destroying the stability of society and plunging it into chaos and anarchy. Flamineo represents an aspect of social inequality in his role as the malcontent — another familiar stereotype of Jacobean drama. Bitter and resentful at his father's squandering of his inheritance, he is motivated by the desire to restore his social position and is prepared to use any unscrupulous means to do so.

Religion

There was no separation of church and state, and the leading prelates of the day were as worldly and politically active as their secular counterparts. England had been a Protestant country since Henry VIII's break with the Roman Catholic church in the 1530s, despite a brief return to Catholicism under Mary I. Protestant orthodoxy presented Catholics as ritualistic idol-worshippers, politically and morally corrupt. Anti-Catholic prejudice was enshrined in the law, with draconian punishments available for varying degrees of recusancy, or refusal to embrace Protestant doctrine. England had also been at war with Catholic states such as Spain, whose armada had been triumphantly defeated in 1588, while Catholic conspiracies such as the 1605 Gunpowder Plot reinforced suspicion of those who espoused the forbidden faith. Dramatists who wanted to attack religious corruption and hypocrisy therefore had a convenient scapegoat in European Catholicism, and Spanish and Italian settings were particularly convenient for exploiting the suspicion and contempt in which foreign countries were held. Jacobean tragedy teems with machiavellian cardinals and corrupt Popes, and in a letter of February 1618 the Venetian envoy, Orazio Busino, was outraged at the attitude to the Catholic church displayed in English drama. 'The English,' he asserted, 'never put on any public show whatever, be it tragedy or satire or comedy, into which they do not insert some Catholic churchman's vices and wickednesses, making mock and scorn of him.' Referring to the role of the Cardinal in *The Duchess of Malfi* — an even more corrupt figure than Monticelso, the Cardinal/Pope of *The White Devil* — he concluded that 'all this was acted in condemnation of the grandeur of the Church, which they despise and which in this kingdom they hate to the death.' Perhaps Busino was being over-sensitive. Webster and his audience would have been only too aware that clerical corruption was not confined to the Catholic faith and it seems to have been merely a cover for an attack on more universal social, political, religious and moral ills.

Women in society

Despite the example of Queen Elizabeth, Jacobean society remained firmly patri-archal and, in many respects, misogynistic. Women's choices were almost entirely circumscribed by men, the power exerted by their fathers being taken over on marriage by their husbands. Independent women were another threat to the social fabric, and those who did not display traditional feminine virtues — modesty, chastity, obedience, mildness — ran the risk of public humiliation or worse, such as Vittoria suffers in the play. In *The White Devil*, both Isabella and Vittoria have undergone arranged marriages, and both are condemned by their society for their subsequent behaviour. It makes no difference that Vittoria's husband, Camillo, is a contemptible buffoon, or that Isabella's husband, Bracciano, is engaged in an illicit affair; the expectations are that both wives will remain loyal and faithful to their husbands. It is notable that they are only able to speak up for themselves by adopting 'masculine' qualities: Vittoria through her vigorous courtroom self-defence in which she is forced to 'personate masculine virtue' (III.2.136), and Isabella by adopting Bracciano's own words in asserting her wish for a separation (II.1.254–63). The misogyny of the time is aptly demonstrated by Monticelso's set-piece denunciation of a 'whore' (III.2.78–101), but the play takes a more ambivalent, perhaps more sympathetic view of women. One of Webster's greatest achievements is how he presents Vittoria, for all her vices, as a figure who elicits our admiration. Thus, the play both demonstrates and challenges the attitudes to women prevalent at the time.

Racial attitudes

Like many plays of the period, such as *The Jew of Malta*, *The Merchant of Venice* and *Othello*, *The White Devil* presents a problem to modern audiences in its presentation of ethnic and cultural difference. White-skinned races were regarded as innately superior — a superiority deeply embedded in culture and language. Darkness and blackness were associated with evil, so that facile comparisons could be drawn between skin colour and moral virtue — something implicit even in the play's title. In fact, there was a surprisingly large ethnic minority population in Jacobean England, especially in London, and visits by foreign ambassadors of other races were not uncommon. One notable example was the state visit of the King of Barbary's ambassador and his retinue to the Elizabethan court in 1600. They were, of course, treated with the dignity that befitted their status, but popular interest in the visit was imbued with a sense of their exotic otherness.

In Webster's play there are two Moorish characters, one 'real' and one fake; in fact, the original text also contains a non-speaking role for 'little Jaques the Moor', attending on Giovanni but excised from many modern editions. The 'real' Moor, Zanche, is triply disadvantaged — as woman, as servant, and as non-white; but, of course, in the original Red Bull production she would be no more 'real' than the fake Moor, 'Mulinassar', since she was being portrayed by a white boy actor. Mulinassar is presented in the play with dignity, and welcomed unreservedly to Bracciano's court. Zanche, however, suffers from persistent racial slurs, her black skin constantly equating her with evil. She is 'the infernal' (V.3.217), a 'black Fury' (V.6.227). However, with the same broad vision that enables Webster to challenge the misogyny of his time, he gives to Zanche a sense of racial pride and dignity as she faces death: 'I am proud /Death cannot alter my complexion, /For I shall ne'er look pale' (V.6.229–31).

Decadence, disease and death

The political, religious and moral corruption of the play's world, highlighted by metaphors of physical decay and rottenness, can also be seen as an implicit attack on the court of King James I. Everything was available to those who had the money to pay for it, from titles and posts of responsibility to all the luxuries and excesses of food, drink and sexual appetite. Elaborately fashionable clothing, extravagant entertainment and architectural riches were all used as a means of displaying power and privilege. The lavish celebrations for Bracciano and Vittoria's marriage, including the duelling contest (or 'barriers') staged at the start of Act V scene 3, were typical of such courtly extravagance, which most of Webster's audience would know of largely from second-hand reports.

On the other side of the coin, the Jacobeans lived in close proximity to disease, violence and death. There was a high rate of infant mortality and most people would consider themselves lucky to survive beyond their thirties. Sexually transmitted diseases were rife, and frequent outbreaks of plague devastated the population. Medical practices were limited and ineffectual. Illness, suffering and death were simply facts of everyday life, as were crime and its violent consequences, both for the victims and the perpetrators. To modern sensibilities, public executions were among the most shocking manifestations of state power, with their grimly sophisticated combination of torture and dismemberment carefully calculated to draw out the victim's suffering for as long as possible and combine it with maximum humiliation. Even more shocking, perhaps, is the public's appetite for such spectacle — but then this was a society that found entertainment in inflicting cruelty on animals and visiting asylums to laugh at the inmates.

Webster's deployment of all the conventionally gruesome trappings of revenge tragedy, from poisoned pictures and poisoned helmets to manifestations of madness and multiple murders, is perhaps one of the least original features of the play. Even his persistent use of the imagery of disease and physical decay as an emblem of political and moral corruption was something of a commonplace of theatrical imagery, used in plays such as Shakespeare's *Hamlet*. To us this emphasis on violence and horror, disease, madness and mortality may seem obsessive, but these were inescapable features of everyday experience for Jacobean audiences.

Jacobean theatre

London's first purpose-built theatre was erected in 1576 in Shoreditch by James Burbage. Simply called The Theatre, it marked the start of probably the richest period of dramatic creativity seen in Britain until well into the twentieth century. Previous theatrical companies had had no permanent performance venues, touring their shows to halls, inn-yards and public spaces; they were regarded as vagrants or beggars if they did not have lordly patronage. There was also a tradition of non-professional performances in the universities, and at the Inns of Court.

By the time Webster was at the height of his success, London had a variety of theatrical companies playing across a range of outdoor and indoor theatres. The most prestigious of these companies had operated as the Lord Chamberlain's Men during the last years of Queen Elizabeth's reign; they opened their Globe Theatre in 1599 and acquired royal patronage on the accession of James I, becoming the King's Men in 1603. Their chief rivals were Prince Henry's Men, formerly the Admiral's Men, based at the nearby Rose. Great performers had established popular reputations, from the tragic actors Edward Alleyn and Richard Burbage to the comedians Richard Tarlton and Will Kemp. Two generations of dramatists had provided increasingly sophisticated plays in a variety of genres. Christopher Marlowe, Thomas Kyd and William Shakespeare had established their reputations in the 1580s, and Ben Jonson, Thomas Middleton, Thomas Dekker, George Chapman, John Marston and Thomas Heywood were among those who gained popularity in the early years of King James's reign. Plays such as

Marlowe's *The Jew of Malta* and Kyd's *The Spanish Tragedy* were perennial favourites, and Shake-speare's plays were regularly among those chosen by royal command for performances at court.

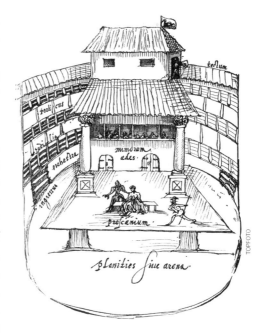

If you have visited the recon-structed Globe Theatre in London, on the south bank of the Thames at Southwark, a few hundred yards from its original site, you may have gained the impression that we know a great deal about the playhouses of Elizabethan and Jacobean London, and how plays were staged there. In fact, we know surprisingly little. Our classic image of an Elizabethan theatre, so vividly portrayed in films such as Laurence Olivier's *Henry V* (1944) or John Madden's *Shakespeare in Love* (1998), is based on calculated guesswork — a set of assumptions and conjectures derived from comparatively limited documentary evidence and a few archaeological remains. Only one contemporary drawing of an Elizabethan theatre, the Swan, survives (reproduced above right) — and that is of somewhat doubtful accuracy.

Some points that are important to understand in order to grasp certain features of the plays of the Elizabethan and Jacobean period are outlined below:

- The public playhouses were open-air amphitheatres holding 2,000–3,000 spectators. They may have been modelled on the inn-yards where plays had often been performed in the past.
- The stage was a raised wooden platform thrust into the yard or pit. It was covered by a canopy, probably supported by two pillars.
- Stage features included a curtained-off alcove or recess at the back, flanked by two doors for entrances and exits, with a balcony above.
- Entrances (and exits) were also possible through a trap-door, and the more sophisticated theatres could fly in actors from above.
- Performances took place in the afternoon, and were lit by daylight.
- Props and furniture were used, but sets were minimal. Setting and atmosphere had to be created where necessary in the words of the script.
- Costumes were splendid and elaborate, but little effort was made to match them to the period of the play; instead, they reflected characters and status.
- Music was an important part of the performance, and there was also a range of sound and other special effects, from thunder to fireworks.

- Women were not allowed to act, so female parts were taken by boys. Some roles, such as the witches in *Macbeth* or the Nurse in *Romeo and Juliet*, were probably played by men.
- Audiences came from all social groups. Those who could afford to pay more sat in the galleries; others stood in the yard.
- Many people in the audience would have had a restricted view of the stage. People generally spoke of going to *hear* a play rather than going to *see* one. The emphasis was therefore on the spoken text.
- Plays were often performed at court by royal command, and they could be adapted easily to different venues.
- There were a number of private indoor theatres, lit by candles, which catered for a more educated, courtly audience. These were mostly occupied by companies of boy actors.
- The King's Men did not perform regularly in an indoor theatre until 1609, when they opened the Blackfriars as their winter home.
- The needs of the Blackfriars, such as regular intervals for trimming the candles, had an effect on the dramatic structuring of play scripts.

Webster's life and works

Comparatively little is known about Webster's life, partly because of the destruction of many of the relevant parish records in the Great Fire of London in 1666. He was born in 1579 or 1580, the son of a prosperous coach-maker, also named John, who was a member of the Company of Merchant Taylors, one of the most prestigious craft guilds. The family lived at Smithfield in London, near to the site of the annual St Bartholomew's Fair and regular livestock markets. From about 1587, Webster almost certainly attended the Merchant Taylor's School, which was unusual in that it taught English as well as Latin, and it encouraged participation in musical and dramatic performances to promote self-confidence and discipline; some of the students took part in pageants and other civic celebrations.

Webster's professional theatrical career began around 1598, and for a number of years he was employed in collaborative script-writing for the impresario and theatre manager Philip Henslowe. He worked with Thomas Dekker on two satirical and scandalous comedies for the children's company of St Paul's, *Westward Ho!* (1604) and *Northward Ho!* (1605), and was also lucky to work on a commission for the prestigious King's Men, writing an Induction and other additions for a revival of John Marston's tragicomedy *The Malcontent* in 1604. At about this time he married Sara Peniall, who was 10 years his junior, and a son, John, was baptised in 1606.

Webster's career as a writer reached its height between 1612 and 1616, though *The White Devil*, the first of his great tragedies, was initially unsuccessful in the theatre. It was premiered by the Queen's Men at the Red Bull Theatre in Clerkenwell, north London, during the winter season at the beginning of 1612. Like most of the popular theatres of the time, the Red Bull was an open-air venue; unlike the Globe, however, it attracted comparatively unsophisticated audiences with a taste for rather more robust entertainment than Webster's subtle and compex play offered. In a preface to the published text of *The White Devil*, Webster complained that the play was acted 'in so dull a time of winter' in 'so open and black a theatre' that it did not receive 'a full and understanding auditory'. He attacked the Red Bull's regular patrons as 'ignorant asses'. However, he was apparently pleased with the production of the play, and particularly praised Richard Perkins, who probably played Flamineo.

Webster was more fortunate in having *The Duchess of Malfi*, roughly 2 years later, performed by the King's Men, who had been running two theatres since 1609. The Globe was their successful open-air auditorium, where they performed to a socially varied audience in the summer months, while in the winter they operated at the indoor Blackfriars, performing to a more courtly and educated private audience. The original Globe had burned down in 1613, during a performance of Shakespeare and Fletcher's play about Henry VIII, *All Is True*, but was rebuilt immediately, and reopened within a year.

Webster's writing career ranged beyond the playhouse. In 1613 he wrote an elegy on the death of Henry, Prince of Wales, entitled *A Monumental Column*. He also contributed 32 'characters' to the sixth edition of Sir Thomas Overbury's *New and Choice Characters, of Several Authors*. Back in the theatre, his only other substantial surviving play, the tragicomedy *The Devil's Law-Case*, also presumably dates from the same period. By now he was famous enough to be the victim of an entertaining satirical attack in Henry Fitzgeffry's poem 'Notes from Blackfriars', published in 1617, which offered a less than flattering description of the various patrons of the private theatre. In a snide reference to Webster's father's trade, Fitzgeffrey characterised him as 'crabbed Websterio, / The playwright–cartwright', and made fun of his laboured method of composition and the obscurity of his work.

Though Webster lived for another 15 years or so — all we know is that he was dead by 1634 — he never equalled the achievement of his two great tragedies. Harking back to his educational and family background, he was responsible in 1624 for organising the elaborate and spectacular Lord Mayor's Pageant, produced by the Merchant Taylor's Company. Otherwise, he seems to have reverted to dramatic collaborations, notably *Anything for a Quiet Life* with Thomas Middleton, and *A Cure for a Cuckold* with William Rowley.

Genre: revenge tragedy

Tragedy as a dramatic form dates back to the theatre of ancient Greece. Centred on characters of high social status who suffer calamity as a result of some personal flaw, error of judgement, ignorance of the truth or divine influence, tragedy shows its protagonists achieving dignity and self-knowledge through the suffering they endure. The Greek writer Aristotle (384–322 BC) theorised about the nature of tragedy in his *Poetics*, specifying its effect on the audience as the evocation of pity and fear, emotions which are then purged and purified through what he called catharsis. English Renaissance writers were familiar with Aristotle's theories and inevitably developed their own versions of the tragic genre as theatres and plays became more sophisticated. They diverged from Aristotle particularly in notions of dramatic structure. Aristotle's concept of the unities — 'rules' specifying that a play's action should consist of one unified plot, enacted in one location and taking place within a single day — were consistently flouted. English Renaissance tragedy frequently developed subplots and comic elements, and its action was often temporally and geographically diverse.

One variant, developed by a number of writers during the last 20 years of the sixteenth century, towards the end of Elizabeth I's reign, has come to be known as revenge tragedy. Early examples, which gained great popularity, were Kyd's *The Spanish Tragedy* (1587), Marlowe's *The Jew of Malta* (1589) and Shakespeare's *Titus Andronicus* (1591).

Revenge tragedy remained popular during the first decade of the seventeenth century, under James I. Examples include Shakespeare's *Hamlet* (1600), Middleton's *The Revenger's Tragedy* (1606) and Tourneur's *The Atheist's Tragedy* (1611). Marston's *The Malcontent* (1603) was a form of revenge tragicomedy.

Like all genre classification, the term 'revenge tragedy' covers a variety of diverse plays. However, it is possible to identify some of the key features of the genre, which are listed below:

- characters whose actions are motivated by codes of honour and the desire for revenge
- bloody and violent acts, torture and madness
- elements of the supernatural, including the appearance of ghosts
- settings in foreign countries, frequently Spain or Italy
- an atmosphere of political, moral and religious corruption
- key character types, such as the malcontent and the machiavel
- a mingling of gruesome acts and tragic events with a kind of grotesque comedy
- the sense that the revenger himself is morally corrupted by the very act of revenge

The greatest revenge plays of the early seventeenth century transcend the apparently restricting confines of the genre, offering complex and ambiguous reflections on the nature of revenge and its impact on both its practitioners and its victims. *The Spanish Tragedy* remained a popular theatrical model, but it was parodied as much as it was admired. Its portentous dramatic machinery of ghosts and dumb shows, elaborate rhetoric, assumed madness and theatrical self-awareness was reinvented as part of a more sophisticated approach to the telling of stories of revenge. In *Hamlet*, for example, the visceral, emotional impact of the urge for revenge is replaced by an intellectual, philosophical tone appropriate to a revenger who thinks so much that his revenge is repeatedly deferred as he questions the entire meaning of existence. In other plays, revenge becomes merely one among many motives in the drama, and the revenger is not necessarily the central focus. Many critics therefore consider 'revenge tragedy' to be an unhelpful classification, preferring 'tragedy of blood' as a more appropriate generic term.

Revenge tragedy retained its appeal throughout the Jacobean period, and its greatest exponents were John Webster and Thomas Middleton, whose plays are complex examples of the genre. In *The Duchess of Malfi*, as in *The White Devil*, Webster portrays multiple acts of revenge. Ferdinand and the Cardinal viciously revenge themselves on their sister, merely because she has remarried in opposition to their wishes. Their chief instrument, Bosola, then turns against them to revenge the murder of the Duchess, which he himself was instrumental in committing.

In *Women Beware Women*, Middleton weaves a complex web of intrigue and revenge, presided over by the cynically manipulative Livia and culminating in multiple murders enacted during a celebratory masque. In *The Changeling*, written by Middleton in collaboration with William Rowley, a young bride, Beatrice-Joanna, employs her hated servant, De Flores, to murder her unwanted suitor, but the murderer demands her sexual favours as his reward, thus polluting her subsequent marriage to Alsemero, the man she loves. The passion and vengeance of the main plot are set against scenes in a madhouse, suggesting a world in terminal moral and emotional disintegration.

Revenge tragedies remained popular into the reign of Charles I, with John Ford as the genre's most notable exponent. His first attempt, *The Broken Heart*, is cooler in tone than the tragedies of Webster and Middleton, and less extravagant in its dissection of the revengeful consequences of an enforced marriage. His better-known tragedy, *'Tis Pity She's a Whore*, explores the consequences of an incestuous affair between a brother and sister, Giovanni and Annabella. The famously bloody climax has Giovanni killing his sister–lover and disrupting her husband's birthday feast with her heart on his dagger.

Sources of the play

The plot of *The White Devil* is based on historical events that had taken place within Webster's lifetime. The following is a brief summary in which the historical facts are conflated with the less accurate versions that Webster had picked up from his reading. The more doubtful elements are printed in italics.

- Paulo Giordano Orsini was born in 1537. He later became the Duke of Bracciano.
- In 1553 he was betrothed to the 11-year-old Isabella de Medici, whom he married in 1558. They had three children, the eldest a son, Virginio (Giovanni in the play).
- Vittoria Accoramboni was born in 1557 in Gubbio, a small town about 100 miles north of Rome. She was one of 11 children.
- Her parents, though from an aristocratic family, found it difficult to make ends meet.
- At the age of 16, Vittoria married Francesco Peretti (Webster's Camillo) in Rome. He was the nephew of Cardinal Montalto (Monticelso in the play).
- In 1576 Bracciano discovered that his wife, Isabella, had a lover. She was subsequently murdered, probably by her husband.
- Vittoria and Bracciano met in about 1580, and began an adulterous relationship. Shortly afterwards, Bracciano, with the aid of Vittoria's brother Marcello, had her husband killed, and he married Vittoria in secret.
- *Isabella's murder may in fact have taken place at about the same time.*
- For 4 years, under the orders of Pope Gregory XIII, Bracciano and Vittoria attempted to separate, but were constantly drawn back together.
- During investigations into Peretti's (Camillo's) murder, Vittoria spent some time imprisoned in Castle Angelo in Rome.
- When she was released, she and Bracciano renewed their marriage vows and lived at his fortified palace north of Rome.
- They openly married for the third time in April 1585, on the death of Pope Gregory. On the same day, Montalto (Monticelso) was elected as the new Pope, under the title of Sixtus V (not Paul IV as in the play).
- Bracciano and Vittoria settled first in Venice, then in Padua. He was by now grossly overweight and suffering from a leg ulcer; for his health's sake, they moved to Lake Garda, where he died on 13 November 1585. *There were suspicions that he had been poisoned.*
- Isabella's relatives, supported by the new Pope, were anxious to protect the interests of Bracciano's heir, Virginio (Giovanni). Vittoria was urged to forego the substantial property left to her in Bracciano's will, but she refused.
- Lodovico Orsini, a relative of Bracciano, *who had previously been banished from Rome for multiple murders*, was employed, *possibly by Francisco de Medici*, to direct Vittoria's murder. In late 1585 or early 1586, *her house in Padua was stormed by 50 men, her brother Flaminio was shot, and Vittoria was stabbed at prayer.*
- *Lodovico was apprehended, confessed that he had murdered Vittoria on the orders of great princes, and was executed by strangling. His accomplices were mutilated with red-hot tongs, killed with a hammer and dismembered.*

It is difficult even now to separate the facts of the story from their subsequent embroidery with gossip, rumour and speculation. There are over 100 contemporary accounts of the story in letters and pamphlets, and six versions claiming to be histories of the affair. We have no means of knowing which of these Webster had read; consequently, we cannot assess how much of his own version of events was borrowed directly from his sources, and how much he changed for dramatic effect.

What we can say is that, from his reading, Webster has turned the sketchy and exaggerated figures of history and gossip into impressive, fully-rounded portraits of complex human beings. In particular, he has presented Vittoria as a figure of ambiguously attractive assertiveness, struggling for independence in a stifling patriarchal society, in two entirely original scenes (III.2 and IV.2); and he has conflated the two brothers from the sources into the role of the malcontent Flamineo, the sceptical, self-interested commentator whose feigned madness leads him through fratricide to a growing self-awareness.

The printed text

The White Devil was first published in a quarto edition in 1612, shortly after the play was first performed. This was probably printed from a copy of the play in Webster's own handwriting, and there is evidence that he was involved in proofreading and correcting the text during the printing process. This edition was reprinted in 1631, 1665 and 1672.

Despite the author's involvement, the quarto text is not free from errors, some of which were corrected in later editions. Even with the sophisticated technology of modern publishing, misprints and other errors frequently find their way into the printed copy.* In Webster's time, the printing-house staff, including the compositors who set up the pieces of type, would have felt free to correct and alter the text, following their own particular preferences for spelling and punctuation, but might also introduce mistakes of their own.

The job of a modern editor of the play is to consult all the early printed texts, compare them, and come up with as accurate a version as possible. Where there are problems, different editors will make different choices, which explains why there are often variations between modern editions. Most present-day editors will modernise the spelling and punctuation, but even here alternative choices can arise. The hero's name, for example, is spelt as 'Brachiano' in the quarto text, a spelling followed in the New Mermaid and other modern editions. However, the Revels editor, John Russell Brown, argues that the spelling 'Brachiano' is merely an attempt to indicate how to pronounce the name, and uses instead the correct Italian spelling, 'Bracciano'. However it is spelt, the name should be pronounced as 'Bratchiano'.

Essentially, though, the principal changes made by modern editors are as follows:

- correcting obvious misprints
- altering spelling and punctuation to conform to modern conventions
- identifying apparent errors and difficulties in the quarto text and attempting to provide a reading that makes sense
- rationalising stage directions to give a clearer idea of the action
- adding line numbers to each scene — these may be different in different editions, because lines of prose occupy varying amounts of space depending on the format of the edition and the typeface used

Many of these editorial practices, however, are acts of interpretation as much as clarification, and can have a variety of problematic effects:

- Changing the way a sentence is punctuated can alter its meaning, shift its emphasis or remove deliberate ambiguities.
- Modernising spelling can obscure the Jacobean pronunciation, perhaps eliminating subtle effects of assonance or onomatopoeia.
- Fixing stage directions can limit a reader's awareness of alternative ways of staging a scene.

You should get into the habit of using your edition critically and questioning its assumptions. If you think of the text as a blueprint for a theatrical performance, with all the staging alternatives that this implies, you cannot go far wrong.

*The Revels Student edition, used for the references in this Student Text Guide, has its own selection of misprints in the text. For example, at III.2.30 it prints 'extrip' instead of 'extirp'; at III.2.78 it has 'your' instead of 'you'; at III.3 47 it puts 'gentlement' for 'gentlemen'; and at V.1.82 it prints 'Let him to Florence!' instead of 'Led him to Florence!'

Scene summaries and commentary

As with all parts of this guide, you should use this section critically. It is not a substitute for your own close reading of the text: there are other angles and interpretations which are not represented here. Question everything you read and weigh it against your own understanding of each scene. The commentary in particular is highly selective. It cannot cover every aspect of every scene, and the focus here is usually on character, with regular reflections on themes, language and staging.

Act I scene 1

Lodovico, a nobleman, has been banished from Rome, principally for his part in various murders. His supporters, Antonelli and Gasparo, attempt to offer him solace, but he vows revenge on those he blames for his misfortunes, which seems to include the Duke of Bracciano and Vittoria Corombona, whom he suggests have been engaged in an illicit affair.

Webster teases his audience with the opening scene of *The White Devil*, presenting Lodovico in a way that suggests he is to be the play's central character, when in fact he does not reappear as a speaking character until towards the end of Act III. The playwright is demanding a great deal of his audience, in expecting them to remember exactly who Lodovico is when he returns to the action. So, who is he?

Lodovico has been banished from Rome for his part in 'certain murders' which were 'Bloody and full of horror'. However, Antonelli and Gasparo, his friends and supporters, suggest other moral misdemeanours that have deserved punishment from the 'men of princely rank' that are now Lodovico's enemies. In 3 years, Antonelli says, he has 'Ruined the noblest earldom' — presumably his own — through his extravagant and dissipated lifestyle: excessive alcohol, culinary luxuries such as caviare (a new and expensive delicacy) and so on. He has invited scores of acolytes and hangers-on to his 'prodigal feasts' until they have bled him dry and 'Vomit[ed] [him] up i'th'kennel' (meaning the gutter).

Lodovico shows no remorse for his actions — the murders of which he has been convicted were mere 'flea-bitings' to him, a view he justifies by wondering why he was not condemned to death. Gasparo suggests this was because the law does not always punish violence with violence, but has offered him the 'gentle penance' of banishment in the hope of his moral rehabilitation, as a positive example to others. Lodovico, though, is bitterly cynical in his attitude to the powerful men who have condemned him, as well as to 'Fortune' in general. In a vivid metaphorical phrase, he threatens revenge on his enemies: 'I'll make Italian cut-works in their guts / If ever I return'.

Among those attacked in Lodovico's rantings, Webster slips in a specific reference to the play's two central characters; again, he expects the audience to remember this. Lodovico wonders why the Duke of Bracciano has not also been banished, for his illicit affair with Vittoria Corombona, and asserts that 'For one kiss to the duke', Vittoria could have elicited a pardon for him, suggesting, perhaps, some kind of relationship between Vittoria and Lodovico himself. It is not clear who the 'duke' is who is referred to here; it could be Duke Bracciano, who has just been mentioned, or it could be the Duke of Florence, Francisco de Medici, who is to emerge as one of the play's most powerful politicians. Whichever is meant, it is obviously that duke that has sentenced Lodovico to be banished.

Antonelli and Gasparo are characterised as solid friends and supporters of Lodovico in this scene. They are not afraid to criticise him and remind him of his crimes; they attempt to offer solace; and they promise to work in his absence to repeal his banishment. Antonelli seeks to offer particular reassurance, expressing the idea in a pair of moral *sententiae* that Lodovico's banishment may do him good, just as trees produce better fruit after having been transplanted, and perfumes exude their scents more readily when bruised. However, in a vivid phrase, Lodovico condemns these encouraging sentiments as 'painted comforts', one of many phrases in the play expressive of a pleasant but fake outward appearance masking a less pleasant reality — a notion summed up in the play's very title.

Antonelli is not the only character in the scene or, indeed, in the whole play, to express moral, philosophical or political ideas through the use of *sententiae* — neat phrases, usually in the form of a metaphorical analogy and often captured in a rhyming couplet, that sum up an apparent truth. Lodovico himself uses three in his first speech and a number of others later in the scene. Sometimes they can have ironic force, as when he claims sarcastically to pray for his enemies just as 'The violent thunder is adored by those / Are pashed in pieces by it'. Such *sententiae* are a characteristic feature of Webster's style, and are usually not original. Webster was a voracious reader, noted much of his reading in his common-place book, and used it in the dialogue of his plays. In Webster's time such literary 'borrowings' were admired rather than denigrated.

This is a verse scene, and the rhythms of the iambic pentameter are generally regular, giving a thumping impetus to the powerful emotions expressed. Typical of the period, it is blank (or unrhymed) verse, with the conclusion of the scene marked by a rhyming couplet. Particularly notable is the number of shared lines in the scene; indeed, virtually every speech begins halfway through a verse line, with line 53 being split between three speeches. This technique gives a real sense of rapid conversational intercourse, and in performance needs to be delivered fast, with any pauses coming within longer speeches rather than between speeches.

Act I scene 2

Bracciano is departing after a visit to Vittoria and her husband, Camillo. As he is about to leave, Flamineo, Vittoria's brother, tells him his sister will see him privately. Flamineo ushers Bracciano away as Camillo returns, on his way to his separate bedroom. He expresses suspicion of Bracciano's intentions towards his wife, which Flamineo tells him is stupid and groundless. As Camillo observes, Flamineo pretends to berate Vittoria for her attitude to her husband, apparently persuading her to let him sleep with her, but then he advises Camillo not to lie with her that night, as if this would be a punishment to her. Camillo falls for the trick, denies Vittoria his loving attentions, and promises to let Flamineo lock him into his room overnight.

When Camillo leaves, Bracciano returns, and the romantic encounter between him and Vittoria takes place against the domestic comfort of carpet and cushions provided by Zanche, her chambermaid, who is privy to their relationship. However, the liaison is also observed by Cornelia, Vittoria and Flamineo's mother. Vittoria describes to Bracciano a dream she has had which culminated in the death of her husband and his wife. Cornelia intervenes with angry recriminations; she tells Bracciano his wife has come to Rome, and curses Vittoria, who rushes off. Bracciano leaves in anger, blaming Cornelia for any subsequent misfortunes and ordering Flamineo to send Dr Julio to him. Flamineo berates his mother and bemoans his

poverty and social inferiority. Cornelia departs in an emotional state, leaving Flamineo to express his disquiet that Bracciano's duchess has arrived in court and to contemplate the need for devious expedients.

This begins as a comic scene, developing the bawdy comedy of sexual intrigue. Camillo, the stupid, jealous husband who facilitates his wife's adultery in seeking to prevent it, is a stock comic type. However, the controller of the scene's comedy is Flamineo, and his role is in many ways the most rewarding in the play. Following Camillo's exit, however, the scene develops into a tensely dramatic exposé of illicit love and its potential consequences.

While the previous scene functioned as a kind of prologue, this one provides a full-scale exposition, in which most of the play's central relationships are explained and shown in action. Webster varies his style enormously, veering confidently between prose and verse to reflect the changing mood. Flamineo is essentially a prose-speaking character, which is appropriate to his comic function and his subservient status, but he can switch readily into blank verse to give forcefulness to his dialogue with Camillo (lines 48–86), passion to his emotional outburst against his mother (lines 309–45) and intellectual strength to his concluding soliloquy (lines 347–55). He combines the qualities of two stock character-types from the period's drama, the malcontent and the machiavel. He reveals himself at the end of the scene to be discontented with his social position, for which he blames his mother, and burning with resentment that he is reduced to being a mere servant to Bracciano (his 'master' as Camillo earlier calls him). He demands to know from Cornelia where is the 'mass of wealth' she should have saved to enable him to elevate his social position and 'bear [his] beard out of the level / Of [his] lord's stirrup'. He reminds her of the family background and his own upbringing, as a poor student and subsequently Bracciano's servant. It is clear that in furthering his master's relationship with his sister, he is acting in his own interests, seeing this as 'a path so open and so free / To [his] preferment' — which means his advancement or promotion. These are the motives that animate his machiavellian qualities, which become explicit in his final soliloquy and are summed up in its concluding couplet:

> So who [i.e. whoever] knows policy and her true aspect,
> Shall find her ways winding and indirect.

It is this deviousness that marks the machiavellian plotter who works through 'policy' — which means the kind of strategies and machinations through which one's aims are to be achieved. It is interesting that Flamineo's language personifies 'policy' as female in gender, suggesting something of the misogyny of the period in its assumption that deviousness is an inherently female quality.

Webster saves these revelations of Flamineo's true feelings and motives until the end of the scene, however, revealing him first as the consummate actor in a succession of roles: the loyal servant (addressing Bracciano as 'my honoured lord'), efficiently organising the

departure of his master's coach and attendants; the sexually knowing pander, full of bawdy wit; the genial brother-in-law, offering useful relationship-counselling (if in a rather sarcastic tone); and the supportive brother, helping to further his sister's sexual desires. In all these roles he exudes energy, wit, linguistic flair and an attractive air of wickedness, and the audience should relish his supreme manipulative control — especially in the astonishing sequence when he convinces the watching Camillo that he is praising his virtues to Vittoria, while giving her the opposite message in a series of muttered asides (rendered in brackets in the Revels text — see lines 128–44). Yet, throughout Flamineo's speeches, we should be aware of an insistent vein of deeply unpleasant misogyny, expressed both openly ('Her coyness? That's but the superficies of lust most women have; yet why should ladies blush to hear that named, which they do not fear to handle?') and through his insinuating use of sexual innuendo ('I have almost wrought her to it, — I find her coming'), often suggestive of his own underlying incestuous feelings towards his sister. Like Pandarus — the original pander — in Shakespeare's *Troilus and Cressida*, Flamineo seems to derive a vicarious thrill from observing the results of his labours. By the end of the scene, though, we must be clear that he is also cynical, vicious and ruthless — a man who can take delight in his sister's apparent manipulation of her lover into murdering both their spouses:

> Excellent devil!
> She hath taught him in a dream
> To make away his duchess and her husband.

Bracciano makes much less of an impression in this scene. At first he seems to lack confidence in himself; he is 'Quite lost' in his apparent lack of success with Vittoria, and even when Flamineo tells him she will see him, he questions his own merit, worries about 'her jealous husband' and thinks she might 'fail to come'. In his assignation with Vittoria, he seems the weaker of the two emotionally, and is still insecure: 'Loose me not madam, for if you forgo me /I am lost eternally'. When Vittoria recounts her dream, he seems rather obtuse in his interpretation of it, simply claiming it as a sign that he will be her protector from both their spouses and that he will establish her in an unassailable position of power, 'above law and above scandal'. However, assuming he has in fact interpreted the dream accurately, there is no need for him to respond explicitly to its hints of murder. When Cornelia interrupts their tryst, Bracciano is reduced to a spluttering anger, and instead of going after Vittoria he heads petulantly for bed, calling for the doctor and blaming Cornelia for all subsequent misfortune. What makes Bracciano seem weak here is that he merely responds to what happens, rather than initiating it; in performance, however, a virile and attractive actor can invest him with much greater charisma.

At first, Vittoria might seem equally weak; indeed, she only manages four brief inter-jections in the space of the first 94 lines that she is on stage, and an actor in the role has a great deal to convey through her silent responses to her husband and brother. Her initial words to Bracciano's romantic greeting are merely conventional, but the word-play on her 'jewel' makes it clear that the sexual attraction the lovers feel for each other is unlikely to

remain unconsummated for long. It is in her account of her alleged dream that Vittoria's ruthless character is memorably established, however. This is a piece of blatant manipulation, expressed in insidiously powerful verse employing vivid imagery, in which she characterises herself as the victim, 'sadly leaning on a grave', with her husband and Bracciano's duchess as sinister figures armed with 'pick-axe' and 'rusty spade' digging madly at the ground, she 'like a Fury', scattering earth and bones violently around. Both are justly killed, Vittoria concludes, by the yew-tree's falling branch, dislodged in a 'whirlwind'. Flamineo's response to his sister's account of her supposed dream, 'Excellent devil', aptly encapsulates the impression she makes here — beautiful and charismatic, but wicked and evil — and echoes the title of the play. However, she is reduced to brief interjections again by her mother's eruption into the scene, and can only rush off in distress in the face of Cornelia's curses. Vittoria and Bracciano, then, are not presented as conventional lovers: not only is their relationship illicit, but it is already pushing them towards both violence and self-destruction. The language of romantic love is barely heard in this scene; instead, we see sexual passion prefiguring murder.

One of the most striking qualities of the play's world is the extent to which characters spy on each other, emphasised in the frequent use of scenes which are observed by other characters. Here, when Camillo observes Flamineo's conversation about him with Vittoria, he is not seeing and hearing quite what he thinks he is. Subsequently, there are two levels of 'spying' on Vittoria and Bracciano's assignation: Flamineo and Zanche observe openly but make comments to themselves or the audience; Cornelia observes unknown to them all, again adding a commentary for the audience's benefit. In this world, nothing is private, nothing remains secret for long — but observers should not always necessarily believe what they see or hear.

Camillo is a straightforward comic character. The precise degree of sympathy or contempt the audience might have for him will be determined by the qualities a particular actor brings to the role. Cornelia is both a more interesting and more difficult part. It would be easy for her to come across in this scene as a stereotypical ranting old woman, and she can seem comic in performance, but this obscures her status as a rare focus of moral virtue in the play. She is not blameless, and for all we know may well deserve Flamineo's recriminations, but she makes a powerful statement in response to his accusations that stands as the first indication of positive moral values in the play: 'What? Because we are poor, / Shall we be vicious?'. She condemns her daughter and Bracciano's 'violent lust' which has corrupted 'both [their] honours', and makes an impressive statement relating to the example that should be set by the powerful:

> The lives of princes should like dials move,
> Whose regular example is so strong,
> They make the times by them go right or wrong.

Many of her moral statements are couched, as is this one, in the form of emphatic rhyming couplets. Sympathy for her is enhanced by her emphasis on her maternal status: she is horrified to find her 'son the pandar'; bemoans 'the curse of children' who cause both 'tears' and 'fears' in their parents; and, to 'the most woeful end e'er mother kneeled', she curses her daughter. Careful staging and clear, powerful acting is needed for Cornelia's role to have its full moral weight here.

Webster's language in this scene is characteristic of the play as a whole, not just in its easy mingling of prose, blank verse and rhyming couplets, but in its evocative recurring images and its outpouring of metaphorical discourse. Among the key images and motifs of the scene are those relating to the natural world — both peaceful scenes such as the 'summer bird-cage in a garden', and evocations of nature's destructive force: earthquakes, whirlwinds and storms, maggots and mildew. Words like 'policy', 'honour', 'jewel', 'diamond', 'devil' and 'lust' begin, too, to have a cumulative significance.

Act II scene 1

Bracciano's duchess, Isabella, has arrived in Rome with their young son, Giovanni. They are greeted by her brother, Francisco de Medici, with Cardinal Monticelso. Marcello (the brother of Vittoria and Flamineo) announces the arrival of Bracciano, and Isabella urges Francisco to treat him calmly; it is clear Bracciano's relationship with Vittoria is well known.

Isabella departs as her husband enters, and he is left to be questioned by Monticelso and Francisco. They accuse Bracciano of adultery with Vittoria, and Francisco and Bracciano exchange angry threats. The Cardinal calms them, but Francisco then complains that Bracciano has ignored his request for help against the pirates, including the banished Lodovico. The entry of Bracciano's young son, Giovanni, with his childish talk of soldiership, apparently reconciles the brothers-in-law, following which Isabella returns for a private talk with her husband.

Bracciano offers Isabella harsh words, vows never to sleep with her again, and disparages her brother, Francisco. Distraught, she offers to take the blame for their separation on herself, citing her jealousy, and when the others return she convincingly acts the role of the jealous wife, berating her rival Vittoria and swearing never again to sleep with her husband. Francisco blames her for her inexplicable change of heart, and she leaves for Padua.

Camillo arrives and, while he is engaged on political business with Francisco and Monticelso, Bracciano and Flamineo discuss with Doctor Julio the proposed murders of both Camillo and Isabella.

Monticelso and Francisco tell Camillo that he is rumoured to be a cuckold — in other words, his wife has committed adultery. They appoint Camillo and Marcello as joint commissioners for relieving the coast from pirates, and bid them farewell. Francisco and Monticelso then make it clear they have only employed the incompetent Camillo to get him out of Rome, in order to tempt Bracciano and Vittoria into developing their lustful relationship, to lure them into an open scandal that will destroy them. Monticelso reveals that Lodovico, now living in Padua, has applied for a repeal of his banishment, and is intending to approach Isabella for financial support. Francisco and Monticelso relish the prospect of Bracciano's shameful fall.

This is another long and complex scene, which introduces the play's three remaining central characters, Isabella, Francisco and Monticelso, as well as the child, Giovanni. Apart from the plotting of Flamineo, Bracciano and Julio, the scene is entirely in verse, which is again appropriate to the social status of the characters and the passionate nature of the drama. Flamineo is no longer the play's only machiavel, with the devious scheming of Francisco and Monticelso placing them as more politically powerful examples of the same species. Isabella's deviousness in taking on herself the blame for her marital separation is more difficult to assess.

Bracciano makes a much stronger impact here than in his previous scene. Though he prevaricates and seems to capitulate to his wife's powerful friends, it is clear that he remains determined to pursue his relationship with Vittoria by plotting the murders of both Isabella and Camillo. He is probably at his least sympathetic in the dialogue with his son, whom he exploits to patch up an insincere reconciliation with his brother-in-law. Later, he even curses Giovanni, his 'issue', along with the priest who performed the 'wedding mass' between him and Isabella. It is difficult to know how seriously to take Monticelso's flattery of Bracciano when he calls him an 'able' leader who has enhanced his natural capacities with 'High gifts of learning'; however, it is probably important to accept these qualities if we are to view Bracciano as a tragic hero who betrays all his good qualities, as well as his powerful position, to pursue an illicit affair. He remains calm and non-committal in his responses to the Cardinal, but is more aggressive and sarcastic when he invites Francisco to speak, resulting in a virtual slanging-match in which Monticelso has to intervene. 'I am tame, I am tame, sir', Bracciano responds, but we sense his anger still bubbling beneath the surface; thus, his comparison of his renewed friendship with Francisco to 'bones which, broke in sunder and well set, / Knit the more strongly' should probably ring with hypocrisy to the audience's ears.

His conciliatory words vanish as soon as he is left alone with his wife, and he is instantly accusing her of having a lover: she has, he suggests, been 'hurried [...] to Rome' in 'an amorous whirlwind', 'To meet some amorous gallant'. He refuses to kiss her; attacks her for complaining to her brother, whom he insults as 'the corpulent duke'; curses the priest who married them and the son she has borne; and swears never to sleep with her again. Through all this, his language is powerful, vivid and bitter, full of vigorous images and often employing emphatic alliteration and other aural effects. When Isabella unexpectedly says she will take on herself the blame for their separation, he is given little time for reaction — 'Well, take your course' — before the others return, but he falls in with her performance, happy to put himself apparently in the right: 'You see 'tis not my seeking'. If much of Bracciano's role in the scene so far has suggested righteous indignation, his true nature is laid open in his subsequent plotting, taking the first opportunity to quiz Flamineo

and the doctor 'About the murder', which he justifies with the dubious observation, 'Small mischiefs are by greater made secure'. This is a crucial scene in our understanding of Bracciano, and he emerges as a devious, hypocritical, ruthless and powerful pursuer of his own ends, who probably did not even need Vittoria's rather heavy-handed hints in her account of her 'dream' to urge him to the double murder he is planning.

Virtually every character in the play, however, shares Bracciano's devious and ruthless qualities, and even Isabella is presented ambiguously, her motives not entirely open and her behaviour raising many questions. At first she appears virtuous and forgiving, urging her brother and the Cardinal to 'Entreat [Bracciano] mildly' and claiming to have 'freely pardoned' him for his treatment of her. There is, however, something dubious in her imagery as she talks of how her embrace will 'charm his poison', 'force' his obedience and keep him from 'infected straying'; and her agreeing to leave the men to tackle her husband before she sees him herself might be seen to implicate her in their devious methods. When she finally sees Bracciano alone, her amenable greeting is soon turned by his brusque accusations into a series of innuendoes that seem designed to provoke him. It is too easy to take her assertions, 'I will not have you angry' and 'I do not come to chide' at face value, and there is a distinctly disingenuous, if not sarcastic tone to her denial of jealousy: 'My jealousy? / I am to learn what that Italian means'. She seems genuinely shocked, though, when he curses their son ('O, too too far you have cursed'), and her emotional response to his vow to divorce her from his bed carries the weight of true feeling, tinged with understandable self-pity: 'O my winding-sheet, / Now shall I need thee shortly!' However, her motivation in taking the blame for this on herself, to 'work peace' between her husband and her brother, is obscure. Why should she lay herself open to her brother's harsh words, when he accuses her of being 'a foolish, mad, / And jealous woman'? The audience is left guessing, but there is no denying the power of her 'performance', with its vindictive attacks on the adulterous Vittoria (lines 238–51), provoking her brother into claiming she has 'Turned Fury'. There is also something calculating in her repetition of the words Bracciano used to sever himself from her bed (compare lines 194–203 with lines 254–63), and the audience may well withdraw their sympathy from her during this whole sequence. Perhaps, though, Webster is dealing in psychological profundities here: through her performance, it is possible that Isabella finds a way of powerfully expressing what she really feels, letting out her genuine emotional outrage and her vengeful feelings towards Vittoria in a way she could not do more directly. Webster conveys a strong sense of her impotence as a woman in a man's world:

> O that I were a man, or that I had power
> To execute my apprehended wishes,
> I would whip some with scorpions.

As she leaves the scene, there is something genuinely affecting in her final lines, which possibly explain the motivation behind her preceding performance: 'Those are the killing griefs which dare not speak'. Perhaps she has found a subtle way in which to 'dare' to speak in order to relieve herself of those 'killing griefs', by adopting the words of a man, her husband. Typically of Webster, though, there are other hints at work in the scene. Could Isabella's strategy be merely intended to bring about her return to Padua where, we later learn, the banished Lodovico has gone to 'address himself for pension' to her, and where in the next scene we see him '*waiting on her*'? Are we meant to suspect that Bracciano has some justification for suggesting his wife has an 'amorous gallant' — though not, as he suggests, in Rome? In fact, Lodovico later reveals that he 'did love Bracciano's duchess dearly; /[…] / Though she ne'er knew on't' (IV.3.111–13). Perhaps there was more between them than he admits, but Webster has chosen not to enlighten us further, leaving our response to Isabella distinctly ambivalent.

There is less ambivalence, in this scene at least, in our response to Isabella's brother, Francisco de Medici. He works mostly through craft, first by insisting on Isabella's absence for the initial interview with Bracciano, and then by passing the ball to Monticelso, because his own 'heart's too full'. Challenged by his brother-in-law to speak, he is soon reduced to angry and sarcastic accusations and threats: 'We'll end this with the cannon'. Calmed down by Monticelso, he airs some grievances in a more reasonable tone: his applications to Bracciano for aid against 'the pirates', both by letter and in person, have been ignored. Before the argument can be reignited, the appearance of the young Giovanni has a further calming effect, and Francisco seems genuinely affectionate towards the boy, to the extent of asserting his friendship towards Bracciano. Ignorant of what then occurs between Bracciano and Isabella, Francisco turns his anger on her, urging her to 'suffer [her] slight wrongs' with patience, as 'other women' do. He seems, here, to be excusing male adultery, and later suggests that Isabella will come crawling back to the Cardinal for a 'dispensation / Of her rash vow' to forego her husband's bed — a sly dig at women's supposed sexual appetite, which he treats as a cause for 'excellent laughter'. There is something morally distasteful about his attitude in this section.

Later, Francisco turns his attention towards Camillo, Vittoria's cuckolded husband, and, in a rather odd speech, regales him with an allegorical 'tale' (lines 335–56) designed to illustrate how lucky he is to have no children, since any offspring spawned by Vittoria 'Would make both nature, time, and man repent'. In devising Camillo's appointment as joint 'commissioner / For the relieving our Italian coast / From pirates', Francisco is, as ever, in league with Monticelso, securing Camillo's absence merely to trap Vittoria and Bracciano into further lustful assignations. This, of course, reveals his previously expressed reconciliation with his brother-in-law as a complete sham, and his motive is now revealed to be to trap Bracciano into 'notorious scandal' with nothing to 'repair his name', in other words restore his noble reputation. Bracciano must be made to suffer 'deathless shame', so that he and his lover will 'both rot together'. Here, Francisco's motives are revealed in all their tawdry corruption, and there is nothing that suggests his actions are actually on behalf of his sister, rather than merely aimed at defending his own honour and ridding himself of a powerful rival.

Francisco and Monticelso work closely together in their machinations in this scene, an effective machiavellian double-act. The Cardinal's role is to be reasonable, self-controlled and righteous, and he is appropriately well-stocked with moral aphorisms. He

is careful to appear as a neutral negotiator of peace between the warring brothers-in-law, and appeals to Bracciano's fatherly instincts in urging him to be a 'pattern', or moral example, to Giovanni in his own behaviour. In the early part of the scene, the audience may well be taken in by Monticelso's outward demeanour of calmly reasonable exhortation, but by the end his devious purposes are clear. The 'emblem' he shows to his nephew Camillo, apparently 'thrown in at [his] window', which labels him a cuckold, is presumably a device crafted by himself, and he treats the wronged husband with a kind of pseudo-affectionate contempt, getting him out of the way for a 'change [of] air' supposedly intended to ameliorate his status as cuckold — though, as Camillo wryly points out, his absence may simply encourage his wife to further adultery. Monticelso's contempt for Camillo is made clear on his departure, and at last his motives are fully opened for our perusal as he is left alone with Francisco. In a key speech, he defends the apparent dishonour of 'play[ing] thus with my kinsman', claiming 'revenge' as a greater good than protecting the life of the 'brother' on whose behalf the revenge is being pursued. It is not unusual to find such a corrupt churchman in the drama of Webster's time, particularly in the context of a Roman Catholic culture largely despised in Protestant England, when the Pope was regarded virtually as Antichrist. In his subsequent tragedy, *The Duchess of Malfi*, Webster created an even more disturbing portrait of an Italian cardinal.

Giovanni, Bracciano and Isabella's young son, is given a substantial role in the scene. Like young boys in other plays of the period, such as the doomed princes in *Richard III*, Macduff's son in *Macbeth* or Mamillius in *The Winter's Tale*, he is knowing and witty beyond his years, in a way that modern audiences can often find irritating. This child is obsessed with military service; in his first words, he reminds his uncle, Francisco, that he had promised him 'a horse / And armour', and his subsequent dialogue is entirely of soldiership, envisaging himself at the head of an army, leading his troops bravely and treating his prisoners nobly. He shows sexual precocity, too, in asserting that he will reward his soldiers by marrying them to wealthy widows and ensure their subsequent service by conscripting the women into the army. Should we admire a young boy obsessed with fighting? In Webster's time, perhaps; there is at least a sense in which the child's naïve reflections on military matters form a refreshing contrast with the political deviousness and murderous plotting that surround him.

Finally, a character easily passed over in the scene is Marcello. Although he only has four lines, it is important that he makes an impact on stage. He is apparently Francisco's loyal adjutant, highly enough regarded to be entrusted, jointly with Camillo, with ridding the coast of pirates — a task he is 'much honoured' to undertake. What Webster does not reveal at this stage is that Marcello is actually the brother of Vittoria and Flamineo; perhaps in staging the scene, there could be some physical acknowledgement between Marcello and Flamineo, who are on stage together for nearly 100 lines. Thus, one brother is the loyal servant to Bracciano, the other to Francisco, setting up the possibility of divided loyalties; this, however, is something Webster does not allow us to anticipate at the moment, simply by not revealing Marcello's connection with his siblings. By modern standards of dramatic construction, this seems odd.

By the end of this scene, the play's exposition is complete. All the main characters have been introduced, the relationships between them established, and various strands of the narrative set in motion. We are anticipating two murders and their consequences; further developments in the relationship of Bracciano and Vittoria and the plots laid against them; and some follow-up of the references to the banished Lodovico. In addition, key images of the play have been established and a variety of themes — love, lust, revenge, political corruption, moral virtue — put forward for consideration. Probably, though, we are not quite ready for what Webster pulls out of the hat in the next scene.

Act II scene 2

In Camillo and Vittoria's house, Bracciano has employed a conjurer to reveal to him the manner of Camillo and Isabella's murders. Isabella dies when she kisses Bracciano's portrait, which has been poisoned by Doctor Julio. Camillo has his neck broken by Flamineo in what is made to look like a vaulting-horse accident. Francisco and Monticelso arrest Flamineo and Marcello, who was also present, on suspicion of Camillo's murder, and head off to apprehend Vittoria. Having observed all this in the conjurer's visions, Bracciano makes a hasty exit from the house.

Dumbshows in drama had largely gone out of fashion by the time Webster wrote *The White Devil*, though playwrights still employed them for specific purposes. They provide an opportunity for action and spectacle, usually accompanied by music (see line 36), and had something in common with the court masques popular at the time. Perhaps in this play they were intended to appeal to the rather unsophisticated audience at the Red Bull. They were evidently performed in a stylised manner, with exaggerated gestures and facial expression; this is suggested here by directions such as '*sorrow expressed in* GIOVANNI *and in* Count LODOVICO', '*compliment who shall begin*', and '*wonder at the act*'. Having the dumbshows conjured up magically for Bracciano enables Webster to introduce a sinister supernatural element that will become increasingly important in the play; and to enhance the sense of characters observing or spying on others, already noted in the commentary on Act I scene 2.

In addition, the staging of this scene enhances the play's metatheatrical elements, with 'performances' of various kinds being presented for others, as in the previous scene where Isabella promises to 'perform this sad ensuing part' with a 'piteous […] heart' (II.1.224–25). Here, key words of metatheatre, such as 'show' and 'act' are employed, while the conjurer summons music appropriate to the genre, creating 'a tragic sound'. Webster's prime aim, however, must have been to achieve dramatic compression. To have shown the murders in fully dramatised scenes would have taken too long, when in fact the audience only needs to know they have taken place. The artificiality of the dumbshow also avoids eliciting sympathy for the victims, since the focus of the play's tragic impact is to lie elsewhere.

Webster's presentation of the conjurer is worthy of comment. Though he claims genuine magical powers, as opposed to the kind of cheats and conmen he attacks in his first speech, he claims that he is reluctant to use them, does not like being considered a 'nigromancer', or practiser of the black arts, and has only been persuaded to this demonstration by Bracciano's 'bounty'. Perhaps, like the apothecary in *Romeo and Juliet* who breaks the law by selling Romeo poison, he desperately needs the money. The conjurer's verse is fairly regular and measured, and is free from Webster's typical metaphorical flourishes. There is a sense of bitterness towards those who give his 'art' a bad name by fraudulent practices, culminating in the sarcastic alliteration of 'figure-flingers' to describe horoscope makers. Not unnaturally, his language is packed with the imagery of his trade — spirits, devils, 'juggling tricks', 'almanac-makers' and so on. He clarifies the dumbshows for Bracciano's benefit in an entirely unemotional, factual style, but when Bracciano leaves he does allow himself a moral comment, implying that the duke is one of those 'great men' who does 'great harm' rather than 'great good'.

Act III scene 1

Francisco and Monticelso briefly discuss Vittoria's forthcoming trial. Though there is only circumstantial evidence against her, they believe the presence of all the foreign ambassadors at the trial will be sufficient to blacken her reputation abroad. Flamineo and Marcello are under arrest; Flamineo exchanges bawdy jokes with a lawyer, and Marcello rebukes him for his involvement with Bracciano and Vittoria. Flamineo and the lawyer make sarcastic remarks about the foreign ambassadors as they go past on their way to the trial.

This odd little scene could be omitted without much impact on the plot of the play, though it does serve a number of purposes. It gives an impression of the bustle and activity preceding Vittoria's arraignment, with a sense of the political importance that is being attached to it; again, Monticelso is revealed as a shrewd operator with considerable political influence, though it is not made absolutely clear why he is eager to make Vittoria 'infamous / To all [the] neighbouring kingdoms'. More importantly, the scene establishes Marcello for the first time as Flamineo and Vittoria's brother, and expands on his moral credentials. He has already been referred to as 'good Marcello' (II.1.366) and 'The virtuous Marcello' (II.2.43), and it is now clear how much he disapproves of Flamineo's involvement as pander to Bracciano and their sister. Flamineo gives him little chance to speak, but he does finally assert himself — 'I'll interrupt you' — to urge virtue and honesty on Flamineo in place of 'every politic respect', in other words the motivations of financial and courtly advancement that his brother has been citing in defence of his actions. Such motives, Marcello argues, morally 'infect' those who follow them, even 'where they most advance' them. In this short scene, Marcello is solidly aligned with the moral virtue previously espoused by Cornelia, the mother of these contrasting siblings, while Flamineo simply emphasises the urge for 'preferment' and 'reward' (a word he uses twice), already established in Act I scene 2, that drives him on. He speaks to his brother with some contempt. In his bawdy and sarcastic dialogue with the lawyer, Flamineo displays his usual darkly frivolous, sexually charged wit, but claims that on this occasion it is merely a 'feignèd garb

of mirth /To gull suspicion'; presumably he thinks his lack of outward concern will be seen as a mark of innocence. At any rate, it supports one of the play's central images: the discrepancy between outward appearance and inner reality.

Act III scene 2

The courtroom fills up for Vittoria's trial. Bracciano, who has not been expected, seats himself on a rich cloak on the floor. A lawyer opens the case against Vittoria in Latin, but she insists he abandons this for the sake of comprehension by everyone in the court. He continues in such pompous and affected language, however, that Francisco dismisses him and Monticelso takes over the presentation of the case. He accuses her at length of being a whore and, with Francisco, implies her collusion in Camillo's murder, which she denies. Bracciano admits he was at Vittoria's on the night of Camillo's death, to offer her comfort and advice, and he storms out of the court with blustering threats after accusing Monticelso of lies and hypocrisy. Francisco urges Monticelso to drop the murder charge for lack of proof and concentrate on Vittoria's adultery with Bracciano, for which evidence is produced. She defends herself vigorously and attacks Monticelso for acting as both accuser and judge. Marcello and Flamineo are bailed and Vittoria sentenced to confinement in a detention centre for penitent whores, to which she is duly removed, casting a flurry of bitter words at Monticelso as she goes. Bracciano briefly returns with cryptic words of friendship towards Francisco, and Flamineo interprets this to himself as his master's cunning prelude to the revelation of Isabella's death. He leaves, determining to feign madness on account of his sister's disgrace. The young prince, Giovanni, enters, accompanied by Lodovico, and tells Francisco and Monticelso of Isabella's death.

This wonderful scene achieves the astonishing feat of presenting Vittoria, the adulterous wife and instigator of two murders, as the innocent victim of a devious political system and the admirably outspoken critic of hypocrisy and corruption. As we watch her in action and listen to the vivid power of her language, we are easily persuaded of her almost heroic status. Even after a moment's thought has reminded us of her true nature — the 'devil' behind her outward whiteness — she remains a splendidly impressive figure against the bitter spitefulness of Monticelso and his cronies, who are eager to turn her into a scandalous public spectacle.

Webster begins to direct our response to her through her interaction with the lawyer — possibly a different character from the lawyer of the previous scene. Her boldness in demanding that her case is not conducted in Latin, on the grounds that she wants 'all this assembly' to hear the evidence against her, suggests that she has nothing to hide. Her choice of words is subtle — 'what you can charge me with' suggests that there is very little that can be attested against her. As the lawyer launches into his case in comically pompous and affected language, Vittoria by contrast appears dignified and reasonable, deflating the

lawyer with admirable wit. Francisco has little choice but to dismiss him from the court; however, this does give Monticelso the opportunity to seize control of the prosecution.

Vittoria, however, outmanoeuvres the Cardinal in presentational skill — what we would these days call 'spin'. She twists his opening words to assert her own 'noble' blood, attacks his dual function as cardinal and lawyer, and pointedly condemns his lack of 'charity'. In response to his extensive characterisation of a whore, she merely declares, 'This character 'scapes me'. Webster directs our response through the words of the English ambassador, who notes that 'the cardinal's too bitter'. Monticelso fares no better in adding the accusation of 'Murder' to that of 'Adult'ry'. Her simple denial, her humble appeal to the foreign ambassadors and her courage in the face of a possible death sentence all contrive to support the positive impression she creates, again leading the English ambassador to let fall an admiring remark: 'She hath a brave spirit'.

Bracciano's intervention does not help her case; however, it allows her, left alone with no 'champion', to appear even more sympathetic — a victim of the 'wolf' and the 'poison' that threaten her. Astutely, Francisco drops the murder charge and Monticelso produces Bracciano's letter to Vittoria as evidence of her lust; she, however, evades the charge while maintaining her innocence, claiming she replied to Bracciano's lustful overtures with a 'frosty answer' of which they are unaware. When she suggests to them that shooting flies would be a nobler occupation than persecuting her, we tend to agree. Vittoria's clinching argument is undeniable, as she attacks Monticelso for the blatant unfairness of acting as both her accuser and her judge. He is left to resort to bitterly grudging recriminations about the circumstances of her marriage to his nephew, Camillo, and to impose a sentence on her based on the mere assertion of her guilt, rather than actual proof.

Vittoria's reaction to her sentence of confinement to a 'house of convertites' reduces her to angry sarcasm and threats of 'vengeance', as if she has indeed 'turned Fury'. However, she does not lose our sympathy; her enemies have indeed 'ravished justice', if only because they have completely mishandled their case and allowed her to gain the moral high ground. Her final speeches in the scene restore her dignity, as she refuses to weep and determines to rise above her punishment, making the house of convertites an 'honester' place by her very presence. Her concluding couplet, comparing herself to a diamond spreading its 'richest light' through the darkness, is a ringing endorsement of her whole demeanour throughout the trial, and it would not be surprising if it were received in the theatre with a round of applause. Even if we recall, at this point, Vittoria's guilt and moral corruption, she still seems more impressive than the court that has condemned her with its devious, sordid, spiteful machinations.

Perhaps one of the reasons for our positive response to Vittoria might be the unfairness of her standing trial alone, without any charges being officially levelled at Bracciano. His role in the scene is distinctly ambiguous and not entirely supportive of his lover. There is something arrogant about the way he sits on his rich cloak when told there is no place for him in the courtroom, and then leaves it behind with contemptuous words for the Cardinal. He thus makes himself an ostentatious visible presence through the first half of the trial, even though he does not speak. When he does choose to intervene, it is to defend himself as much as Vittoria, imputing noble motives to himself for his presence at her house on the night of Camillo's murder. However, he is soon drawn into angry and threatening recriminations, accusing Monticelso of injustice and hypocrisy, and his departing Latin words are a direct threat: 'No one injures me without punishment'. He abandons Vittoria to her fate without ever directly standing up for her in the face of the court's accusations, and our admiring response to her is partly the result of Bracciano's inadequacy as her partner in love and crime. When he returns briefly at the end with mysterious words of friendship towards Francisco, we can merely see again how he is conniving at his own protection prior to the revelation of Isabella's death.

Monticelso and Francisco are again contrasted effectively in this scene, but now it is the former who is emotional and obsessive, the latter who is more practical and realistic. It is difficult to assess the extent to which their conduct of the case is pre-planned; even the dismissal of the inadequate lawyer could be part of their strategy, having perhaps antic-ipated Vittoria's objections to him. Monticelso certainly seems well prepared to take on the prosecution. Though his demeanour at the start is outwardly calm, his linguistic choices are calculated to create the worst possible impression of Vittoria, presenting her as an object of scandalised fascination: 'Observe this creature here'. Her 'trade' is that of 'whore'; she is (frequently) a 'devil', showing 'scorn and impudence' as well as 'cunning'. He objects to her social aspirations as much as her moral faults: 'she did counterfeit a prince's court' and is a 'counterfeit jewel', suggesting the deceptiveness of outward appearances crys-tallised in the play's title. Always, he asserts, she has been 'a most notorious strumpet'.

There is something disconcerting, though, about Monticelso's descriptions of Vittoria's lust, and his own language can be used by a skilful actor to suggest that he is barely in control of his own lustful urges: note the relish with which he describes the prospect of 'wanton bathing and the heat / Of a lascivious banquet', and the passion with which he 'expound[s]' to the court the nature of a typical whore. This speech (lines 78–101) is worth noting. It falls into a familiar literary genre of the period, the 'character', in which the qualities of a particular character type are set out. Webster later contributed 32 such 'characters' to the sixth edition of Sir Thomas Overbury's *New and Choice Characters, of Several Authors*; among them were 'A Pirate', 'A Virtuous Widow', 'A French Cook', 'An Excellent Actor' and 'A Purveyor of Tobacco'. The Cardinal's account of a 'whore' works like a kind of inverted blazon — a type of love poem in which a woman's qualities are catalogued in a series of elaborate metaphors. Here, there are a dozen such metaphors, mostly centred on the difference between outward appearance and inner reality, one of the play's central themes. Whores are 'Poisoned perfumes', 'Shipwrecks in calmest weather' or 'counterfeited coin'. More elaborately, they are like incorrectly copied legal documents that bankrupt those they should enrich; or bells that sound identically at both weddings and funerals; or wealth gained by extortion and lost in dissipation. The speech is crammed with references to the ills of society, appropriately perhaps for a churchman. Put in context, however, we can see how Monticelso himself is engaged in the

kind of legal and social injustice and corruption he is here condemning. When Vittoria claims his accusations are merely 'feignèd shadows' of her evils and asserts her immunity to his conjuring of 'painted devils', the phrase is clearly intended to refer back to him; the 'names / Of whore and murd'ress [...] proceed from you', she suggests:

> As if a man should spit against the wind,
> The filth returns in's face.

Francisco is a calmer, more controlled presence in the scene. He dismisses the hapless lawyer with a quiet, sarcastic wit; he explains concisely the circumstances of Camillo's death; he later suggests dropping the charge of murder for lack of evidence; he claims to find it difficult to believe Vittoria could have 'a soul so black' as to commit murder and calmly anticipates that, if she is indeed guilty, time will punish her; he bails Marcello; and he responds with dignified grief to the news of Isabella's death. Webster shows considerable dramatic skill in creating Francisco here: his calmness allows us to focus on the confrontation between Monticelso and Vittoria, but we should also sense that he is calculatedly suppressing his genuine feelings and motives. After all, we already know what he is like when he loses his self-control.

There is much else in this rich scene that is worthy of comment. It deserves close and detailed reading and rereading.

Act III scene 3

Following his resolve to feign madness, Flamineo engages in distracted conversation with the foreign ambassadors and then with Marcello. Observing him, Lodovico is suspicious, while Flamineo in turn wonders why Lodovico has accompanied Giovanni to Rome. They exchange cynically witty remarks until Antonelli and Gasparo enter, laughing; Antonelli informs Lodovico that the Pope, on his deathbed, has signed his pardon, urged to do so by Francisco de Medici. Lodovico then openly condemns Vittoria as a whore and an argument develops, culminating in Flamineo striking Lodovico. Marcello escorts his brother away. Left alone with his companions, Lodovico fumes with rage.

There is more going on in this scene than meets the eye, though, like Act III scene 1, it does little to advance the plot. We are, however, given some crucial information, and Lodovico is re-established as a key player. Most important for future developments are the Pope's imminent demise, and Francisco's advocacy of Lodovico.

Flamineo's feigned madness is worth a closer look. Traditionally, mad characters in drama are made to speak truths, commenting satirically on social ills and the problems of life; Shakespeare's King Lear is a notable example. Flamineo's assumed madness is more controlled, more rational than that of many such characters, and really amounts to an extension of his malcontent's bitterness and cynicism, commenting on a wide range of examples of worldly misery and the hypocrisy of the powerful; a few examples from the scene will serve to demonstrate this. He reflects on the corrupting power of the 'cursed mineral', money — 'there's nothing so holy but money will corrupt and putrify it', he says, implying that the Cardinal himself has succumbed to bribery. He continues harping on religious hypocrisy, remarking on how religion and 'policy' go hand in hand and, in a strikingly modern observation, noting that 'The first bloodshed in the world happened about religion'. Shifting his commentary to social inequalities, he rails against those with aspirations to gentlemanly status, deriding them as 'so many early mushrooms, whose best growth sprang from a dunghill'. Though such social upstarts gain his contempt, it should be remembered that a key source of his own resentment lies in his lowly social position.

So far, apart from the rhyming couplet of Flamineo's opening lines, the scene has been in prose — the conventional linguistic medium for the outbursts of madmen and malcontents. With Lodovico's comment on Flamineo's ravings, however, Webster shifts the dialogue into verse mode, beginning with the two characters' parallel asides, each questioning the other's motives, and moving into rapid exchanges of varied and flexible verse, its pace marked by the number of shared lines. Marcello's observation, 'Mark this strange encounter', cues the audience into paying close attention to their dialogue, as they at first enter into a kind of malcontents' pact to be 'unsociably sociable'. It is indeed an odd encounter, comic yet tense, as if Lodovico and Flamineo are probing each other's deepest thoughts through this mingled bonhomie and detestation. However, on Antonelli's news that Francisco has secured Lodovico's pardon, Lodovico drops the act and openly insults Vittoria. Flamineo feigns outrage that Lodovico's laughter has broken their agreement to engage in shared melancholy, and strikes him; thus the deviousness of their false personas shatters into open conflict. Lodovico's closing speech, though not directly threatening revenge, is full of violent undercurrents, as he physically 'shake[s]' like an 'earthquake'. 'How did my sword miss him?' he wonders, and we are left to anticipate that next time Flamineo may not escape so lightly.

Act IV scene 1

Francisco and Monticelso discuss how to respond to Isabella's murder. Francisco is anxious to avoid all-out war against Bracciano, and Monticelso advises working instead by craft. Francisco appears to reject this advice in favour of leaving retribution to a higher power; however, he asks Monticelso for the loan of his catalogue of criminals. While Monticelso fetches this, Francisco reveals that he has his own devious plots underway. Monticelso runs through the various types of offender in his black book, and Francisco asks him to fold down the page at the list of murderers. Left alone, Francisco reflects on Monticelso's motives in keeping his book, and summons up Isabella's image to reinforce his revengeful feelings. Her ghost appears briefly, after which he begins to put his plan into operation. He composes a love letter to Vittoria and instructs his servant to deliver it to her or the matron in the house of convertites in the sight of Bracciano's followers.

He determines to bribe Lodovico to be the instrument of his revenge, and anticipates Bracciano's death.

This superb scene shows Webster at his best. It may seem to lack dramatic action, but it
pins down with unerring precision the deviousness and distrust that animate the lives of
the rich and powerful. Francisco and Monticelso both operate by craft, and both are
motivated to desire revenge for Isabella's murder — or more, perhaps, in Monticelso's case,
for the murder of his nephew, Camillo. Yet, though they are allies and have worked subtly
in tandem in their previous scenes, it is here revealed that Francisco does not trust the
Cardinal enough to be open with him about his revengeful plans. Instead, he presents
himself on the moral high ground: 'Far be it from my thoughts / To seek revenge', he claims,
justifying this by citing the suffering his people would undergo if he engaged in open war
against Bracciano. The moral force of his speech (lines 5–11) may perhaps, for a moment,
even convince the audience, and it is reinforced by his wish to avoid 'treacherous acts',
leaving justice and punishment to the 'thunder' of the gods. 'Treason', he claims, 'dies' in
its own machinations. Such moral resolve is powerful, convincing, and presented without
obvious irony, yet if we recall the impression previously created of Francisco, it will come
as no surprise when he reveals that it is nothing but a cynical ploy to keep Monticelso in
ignorance of his true intentions. What is more surprising is the extent of his wariness of
the Cardinal: 'I will not trust thee'; and his contemptuous assessment of Monticelso's inca-
pability of grasping the extent of his deviousness: 'Thou canst not reach what I intend to
act'. He suggests that Monticelso's anger is both quick to ignite and soon quenched,
whereas his own is slow-burning and long-lasting.

The actions of both men, however, are an object lesson in the skills and methods of
the classic machiavellian politician. In the Jacobean sense, a politician is not necessarily
someone in a position of social power and rule, but someone who operates by 'policy' —
the strategies and tactics of achieving your aims through intellectual cleverness rather than
physical strength. Such strategies are explained and promoted by both characters
throughout the scene, from Monticelso's assertion, expressed through a military
metaphor, that 'undermining more prevails / Than doth the cannon' to Francisco's more
literal observation, 'He that deals all by strength, his wit is shallow'. Francisco's analysis
of the purposes to which the Cardinal puts his 'black book' demonstrates such 'policy' in
action. The names in the book have been compiled through 'intelligence' — in other words,
the use of spies and informers. Francisco suggests that the list, or the 'knavish summons'
as he calls it, has been made by one of the Cardinal's officers, recently promoted from a
clerk to a judge, who uses it to 'bribe' those who can afford to pay, whose names are then
deleted, with the Cardinal turning a blind eye to their activities. Those who cannot afford
to pay suffer the consequences. Here, Webster seems to offer ample confirmation of
Flamineo's satirical jibe in the previous scene, 'there's nothing so holy but money will
corrupt and putrify it' (III.3.26–27) — a sentiment extended by Francisco in the statement
that 'Divinity, wrested by some factious blood, / Draws swords, swells battles, and

o'erthrows all good', directly echoing another of Flamineo's earlier comments, 'The first bloodshed in the world happened about religion' (III.3.39–40). The Church does not get a good press in this play.

Francisco's own devious plans are clarified at the end of the scene: he composes a feigned love letter to Vittoria and ensures that Bracciano's 'followers' will see it delivered, thus arousing his jealousy. What Francisco imagines will ensue is unclear, but he has no doubt that it will lead to his enemy's death. The Latin line that ends the scene is worth attending to, suggesting as it does that Francisco, like every machiavel, is prepared to work by any means necessary to achieve his ends, whether divine or infernal. His joke on Monticelso's exit, 'You have left me in the company of knaves', along with the Cardinal's own acknowledgement that 'devils' lurk in his black book, are appropriately suggestive indicators of the moral status of both characters.

It is important to remember, though, that these unsavoury politicians inhabit a corrupt society — something made explicit in the very nature of the 'black book', which retails eleven different types of offender, ranging on the scale of criminality from spies and swindlers to corrupt lawyers and churchmen, and from pirates and panders to cross-dressing bawds and outright murderers. This picture of worldly corruption is emphasised by the scene's pervasive animal imagery, suggesting that bestial behaviour has usurped the nobility of human beings created in God's image.

The dramatic structure of the scene, and its language, are worth considering. It is, appropriately enough, a scene entirely in verse — impressive, varied and flexible in its rhythms, capable of expressing the devious windings of the characters' innermost thoughts and outward utterances. Embedded in this are a number of rhyming couplets, which serve various purposes. Sometimes they embody forceful statements of moral probity (lines 10–11, 26–27) or machiavellian policy (lines 18–21, 131–32); sometimes they sum up a character assessment (lines 41–42) or an account of strategy (lines 86–87, 134–35); finally, a couplet brings the scene to a ringingly ominous conclusion (lines 137–38). As elsewhere in the play, the language is highly metaphorical, here giving the sense of two characters of immense intellectual sophistication and imaginative capacity. Webster's characters seem to think in terms of imaginative parallels, sometimes drawing attention to their comparisons by framing them as similes, but more often couching them in the form of direct metaphors that can challenge comprehension. None is more vivid than the combined metaphor and simile of Monticelso's opening lines:

> Come, come my lord, untie your folded thoughts,
> And let them dangle loose as a bride's hair.

The idea of 'folded' thoughts, wound, knotted or tangled, is an apt emblem for the devious plotting of the machiavel, and links back to Flamineo's analysis of the 'winding and indirect' ways of policy, like the 'subtle foldings of a winter's snake' (I.2.349–55). Virgin brides wore their hair loose — a striking contrast of associations with the less than virgin-like Francisco, even though he later claims 'innocence'. But untying the hair was also a sign of grief or

distress, and as such the image fits appropriately with the Cardinal's urging of Francisco to open up his true feelings in response to his sister's death. There are many such richly evocative metaphors in the scene.

It is notable that, from Monticelso's exit, the scene is effectively a monologue for Francisco of over 60 lines. Mostly, this operates as soliloquy, though it incorporates direct instructions to the servant. Most strikingly, however, it encompasses the appearance of Isabella's ghost. Such is Webster's skill that this monologue is a gift for an actor, moving Francisco's character as it does from his reflections on the Cardinal's methods through the conjuring up of Isabella's image to strengthen his resolve to be revenged, to the practical application of the first stage of his plan and his gloating anticipation of Bracciano's fate. As for the ghost itself, its appearance would not have occasioned any particular surprise or disbelief in a Jacobean audience. For one thing, to most people the existence of ghosts was an accepted reality; for another, ghostly appearances were a familiar feature of the period's drama. What is interesting here is that Webster almost goes out of his way to deny the ghost's literal existence and present it as a figment of Francisco's imagination which he conjures up consciously and deliberately to feed his thoughts of revenge — though her image is so vivid it surprises even him. In performance, it would be perfectly acceptable for the ghost not to appear; after all, Francisco's lines do all that is needed to tell the audience what he is seeing. Whatever decision a director takes, it is important to stage the scene with quietness and subtlety; this is not a ghost that needs to be accompanied by lurid lighting, the clanking of chains, a countenance ravaged by poison, or ominously melodramatic music.

Act IV scene 2

Flamineo is arranging access for Bracciano to visit Vittoria, with the reluctant matron of the house of convertites. Francisco's servant delivers his master's feigned love letter to Vittoria, which Flamineo intercepts and reads to Bracciano. Bracciano takes the letter at face value and flies into a fury, threatening violence towards Vittoria; as she enters, he upbraids her, but she denies any relationship with Francisco and claims that it must be a plot. Bracciano repents his relationship with her and chastises her, but she responds with tearful recriminations. With Flamineo's intervention, a certain calm is restored and Bracciano kisses Vittoria, but she remains sullen and silent. Flamineo and Bracciano plot her escape from detention, and Flamineo urges her to show gratitude to Bracciano.

The plots instigated by Francisco in the previous scene come to imminent fruition at the start of this, but not quite as he had planned. Bracciano's jealousy is certainly aroused, but is assuaged by Vittoria's tears and Flamineo's energetic mediation. In fact, Flamineo is restored in this scene to his controlling role in his master's and sister's relationship. It is not entirely clear how much of his assumed madness he retains here, though at the end he justifies to the audience his continuing to 'talk knave and madman', so that it is up to the actor to decide how far this should be played up in the scene. There is an element of complacency in Flamineo's handling of events: twice he attests that the Pope's imminent demise and the subsequent papal election will distract those in power from paying too close attention to the secureness of Vittoria's detention (see lines 4–6, 211–17); we may feel, however, that there will still be eyes on Bracciano and his lover. Otherwise, there is little new to say about Flamineo in this scene: he still energises the dialogue with his cynical wit, indulges in vivid and distasteful language, plays the other characters off against each other with his characteristic skill, and veers flexibly between prose and verse. Most notable is the prose fable he regales the lovers with at the end of the scene. The symbiotic relationship between the crocodile and the bird that picks the worms from its teeth was used as a commonplace moral allegory, however dubious it may be as a piece of natural history. Flamineo craftily manipulates it, though, so that its application is ambiguous. Bracciano's interpretation, that he has not rewarded Flamineo's service, is undoubtedly intended by Flamineo, with an implied threat suggested by the bird's sharp quill, which is left unexplained: does Flamineo mean he could easily harm Bracciano and effect his own escape if necessary? Craftily, though, Flamineo re-applies the moral, claiming it is about Vittoria's ingratitude rather than Bracciano's — again, with the unspoken suggestion that the duke has it in his power to do her harm and make his escape if she does not soften her attitude. The subtextual subtleties here, though they seem obscure, would not be difficult for actors to convey on stage; the main point of the fable, however, is to illustrate the interdependence of these three characters.

Neither Bracciano nor Vittoria emerges well from this scene, though she gains rather more sympathy as the victim of his unfair and intemperate suspicions. Even before hearing Francisco's letter, Bracciano is threatening violence — 'I'll open't, were't her heart' — and assuming the worst about Vittoria's 'juggling', or sexual incontinency, which to him is 'gross and palpable'. His lack of trust in her explodes into explicit threats expressed in the vivid imagery of natural forces prevalent throughout the play:

> I'll cut her into atomies
> And let th'irregular north-wind sweep her up
> And blow her int'his nostrils.

For him, she is now defined by the term society has already chosen for her: 'whore'; or, less explicitly, she is 'changeable stuff' — a phrase that removes her humanity. Like a whore, he anticipates she will infect him with some sexually transmitted disease, of which one symptom was loss of hair; intemperately he offers to tear out his hair before this happens. His anger, threats and insults are directed as much towards Flamineo, whom he blames for bringing them together, as towards Vittoria herself. Flamineo stands up for himself with some vigour, suggesting that he and Bracciano are merely devils of different degree, managing to get in a sly comment about his lack of reward: 'You're a great duke; I your poor secretary'. When Vittoria enters, Bracciano continues his accusations to her face, again imputing to her the characteristics of a whore. He is distracted, though, by her beauty, which he curses for having led him to his 'eternal ruin', asking, in a striking image that clearly alludes directly to the play's title, 'How long have I beheld the devil in crystal?' — suggesting that he has been dazzled by the outward beauty that deflects attention from her inner evil. As so often in the drama of the time, a flawed woman is seen as a microcosm of the whole gender: 'Woman to man / Is either a god or a wolf'. Such misogynistic sentiments were commonplace, and are echoed in the scene by Flamineo: 'What a damned imposthume [abscess] is a woman's will!' he exclaims; 'Can nothing break it?' Later, commenting on Vittoria's rebuking of 'dissembling men', Flamineo claims this is a quality men have 'sucked […] / From women's breasts, in [their] infancy'. The misogyny here, though, is that of the characters, and we need not attribute such sentiments to the play as a whole, nor its author.

Continuing his assault on Vittoria, Bracciano plays the guilt card, hypocritically recalling his 'sweetest duchess', 'whose death God pardon'. This is the spur to Vittoria's retaliation; so far her attempts to defend herself have been limited by her initial ignorance of the contents of the letter, and then by Bracciano's unstoppable fury. Now, though, she asserts a superior moral position and presents herself, in a powerfully emotional speech, as the victim of Bracciano's lust. She blames him for the 'infamy' she has gained, for staining the honour of her family, for bringing about the social exclusion she has suffered and for sending her to this 'house of penitent whores'. Her tone is bitter, superior and sarcastic as she urges her point in a rapid series of rhetorical questions. Then she becomes defiant, dismissing him as a serial womaniser and rejoicing in their inevitable parting, describing him as an ulcerated limb that she has happily amputated. Finally, she resorts to self-pity, wishing for a speedy death and suppressing the tears with which she is racked because he is not worth them.

An actor in the role will need to decide how far Vittoria's response is genuine, spontaneous and sincere, and how far it is a calculated performance for emotional effect; as we saw in her two previous scenes, she is a skilful manipulator of her own image, arousing our admiration in the face of what we know of her actual behaviour. Her passionate speech, culminating in the rather melodramatic action of 'throw[ing] herself upon a bed', certainly has the desired effect. In saying 'I have drunk Lethe', Bracciano is admitting he has been forgetful of his love for Vittoria, and his language becomes affectionate and consoling; he swears that he 'will love [her] everlastingly, / And never more be jealous'. Observe, though, how he appropriates her as his possession — 'Are not those matchless eyes mine? […] Is not this lip mine?' Such language is typically employed to exert patriarchal control. Sensing her advantage, Vittoria resorts to stubbornness; she is not going to be easily won over. Echoing her brother's feelings, she asserts to Bracciano, 'Your dog or hawk should be rewarded better / Than I have been' before launching into her final strategy, 'I'll speak not one word more'. And she doesn't — in this scene, at least. She does, however, allow Bracciano to kiss her and, judging by Flamineo's comments — 'So, now the tide's turned the vessel's come about' — there is some physical indication in her demeanour that she and Bracciano will indeed 'Couple together' once the scene has ended. All that remains is for Vittoria's enfranchisement from the house of convertites to be plotted — disguised as a boy and whisked off by horse and by boat to Padua, accompanied by her mother and both her brothers — that is, if Marcello can be persuaded. Bracciano, meanwhile, will head for Padua separately with his young son. As a sign of his faith, Bracciano offers marriage to Vittoria, urging her to 'Think of a duchess' title', and promises social advancement to the whole family. Perhaps Flamineo's subsequent fable indicates that he is not entirely convinced by these promised outcomes.

Webster's language in this scene follows its familiar track: vivid metaphorical pictures, insistent imagery of animals and birds, disease and corruption. There is one other recurring image cluster that deserves consideration — not exclusive to this scene, but particularly noticeable here. This is the imagery of water and water-borne transport, beginning with Flamineo's comment that Vittoria is 'o'er head and ears in water'. There are references to whirlpools; tears and weeping; the sea; rivers, including Lethe, the river of forgetfulness, and the Nile; a melting snowball; and the turning tide. Flamineo's extended metaphor in which he compares the 'rough and raging sea' to 'calm rivers', concluding that 'A quiet woman / Is a still water under a great bridge. / A man may shoot her safely' gives some indication of the purpose of these images — as well as, incidentally, asserting another misogynistic commonplace. Water in all its forms is infinitely varied, the great shape-changer that moulds its form and mood to geological and meteorological conditions. It is thus an apt metaphor of transformation, suggesting the rapid emotional shifts that take place during the scene as well as the characters' ability to alter themselves according to circumstance. Sometimes in this play the characters seem quite different in different contexts, lacking what we would these days call psychological consistency. They are shifting, unstable, unpredictable; their true nature is hidden, their motives and under-currents obscure — as in Flamineo's 'varying of shapes' which he celebrates at the end of the scene. The watery images are thus cumulatively suggestive of human personality and how difficult it is to grasp.

Act IV scene 3

Under Francisco's instructions, Lodovico is guarding the conclave of cardinals that is electing a new Pope, and supervising the delivery of their food, which is turned away because they have reached a crucial point in their deliberations. The Cardinal of Arragon announces that Monticelso has been elected Pope, with the title of Paul IV. A servant informs Francisco that Vittoria has fled the city with Bracciano and Giovanni; he reflects that this is the outcome he had intended. He whispers the news to the new Pope as he enters in state, and Monticelso immediately excommunicates Vittoria and Bracciano. Francisco briefly confirms Lodovico's assistance in his plot to murder Bracciano. The new Pope returns and interrogates Lodovico about his relationship with Francisco; Lodovico confesses he loved Isabella and has sworn to Francisco to avenge her murder. Monticelso rebukes him and threatens damnation, convincing Lodovico to give up his role in the revenge plot; however, Francisco sends him a thousand ducats supposedly from Monticelso, which he takes

as a sign that the new Pope did not mean what he said and is giving his consent to the planned revenge.

This striking scene is full of colour and pageantry, against which the revengeful plotting, hypocrisy and duplicity stand out more strongly. Francisco and Monticelso, who were allies, are now opposed in their aims, though not openly, while Lodovico's motivation is laid bare. The visual splendour of the scene, culminating in the entry of the new Pope, seems to prioritise stage spectacle over dialogue, but the characterisation of the scene's three protagonists nevertheless maintains Webster's usual combination of subtlety and linguistic extravagance. Though the conclave of cardinals is kept offstage, Webster uses the bustling activity outside the papal palace — Lodovico's commentary on the foreign ambassadors, the arrival of the dishes of food, and the English ambassador's explanations to his French colleague — to build up to the Cardinal of Arragon's announcement and the formal entry of the new Pope. The ambassadors are gloriously attired in 'several habits', the Cardinal of Arragon in scarlet, and Monticelso himself metamorphosed from cardinal's red to papal white, in full headgear and regalia — a visual *coup de théâtre* that also makes a symbolic statement about his character. Red could be interpreted as the colour of blood and lust, while white represents holiness and purity. The question arises, therefore, as to whether Monticelso's new outward appearance will merely categorise him as another 'white devil', or whether his inner character will have been transformed along with his outer vestments.

As far as we can judge from this scene, the latter seems to be the case: he takes a clear moral stand in excommunicating Vittoria and her lover, distances himself from Francisco's machinations, preaches damnation to Lodovico, and is uncharacteristically outwitted when Lodovico reveals the truth to him under the guise of 'confession' — thus guaranteeing that the Pope can neither reveal it nor act on it. As he aptly says, with bitter understatement, 'You have o'erta'en me'. Monticelso's language is impressive throughout: his opening speech with its announcement of excommunication is formal, measured and authoritative; his questioning of Lodovico is, in contrast, insinuatingly colloquial and threatening; his forecast of damnation is vividly metaphorical:

> Dost thou imagine thou canst slide on blood
> And not be tainted with a shameful fall?

He leaves with a ringing couplet, yet again emphasising the key imagery of the play in his rhyming of 'evil' and 'devil'. The question is, how far can we believe this new, morally author-itative Monticelso? Is he, as John Russell Brown suggests, merely 'serving his own personal ends by assuming a new outward behaviour in order to be more secure in his newly acquired office' (Revels Student Edition, Introduction, p. 18)? Can this be the man previously shown to be such a machiavel; a man with a 'black book' crammed with the names of murderers and other offenders who might prove useful to him?

Lodovico re-emerges in this scene as a powerful, sinister character, though his detailed knowledge of the foreign ambassadors is not entirely convincing: he sounds rather like a National Trust guide explaining the heraldic emblems in a stately home. He effectively resists the Pope's interrogation, until he has the sudden notion that he 'care[s] not greatly' if he does reveal the truth, cunningly prefacing it with the warning that it must be counted as his religious 'confession', so that Monticelso is duty bound never to reveal it. He explicitly admits his 'hot lust' for Isabella, and confirms that 'she ne'er knew on't', dissipating any early suspicions Webster aroused in our minds that she possibly returned what she saw as his love. The rapid changes in Lodovico in this scene are unpredictable and baffling, and now he is dissuaded from revenge by the Pope's threats of damnation — but also because he had expected his support for revenge on Bracciano on account of Camillo's murder. His final change, though, is manipulated by Francisco with the unsolicited gift of 1,000 ducats, supposedly from Monticelso, provoking Lodovico to a knowing analysis of the 'art' or policy of great men, who have a thousand times more Furies dwelling in their breasts than live in the whole of 'spacious hell'. The irony of this is, of course, that the machiavellianism he is here attributing to the Pope is actually Francisco's. In Lodovico's role in this scene, something of Webster's technique throughout the play is demonstrated, with the characters' surprising shifts of purpose neatly summed up in his line, 'I'll not tell you; / And yet I care not greatly if I do'.

As for Francisco, he too surprises us in the scene. Where we might have expected him to be furious at Vittoria's escape, instead he claims: ''twas this / I only laboured'. Previously, it will be recalled, his intention seemed to be to provoke Bracciano's jealousy, certainly not his elopement with Vittoria. Now, it appears, he relishes the prospect of Bracciano's 'marry[ing] a whore'; as he comments, 'what can be worse?'. It is clear, though, that this blot on the 'fame' of the 'fond duke' is to be merely the prelude to his murder, which he goes on to plot with Lodovico. There is a wonderful irony in the religious imagery he uses in reminding his henchman that he has 'ta'en the sacrament to prosecute / Th'intended murder', and a sinister undercurrent to his admission that he has supporters, spies and informers among Bracciano's followers. His manipulation of Lodovico with the supposed payment from the Pope confirms him as a supreme practitioner of 'policy' — though perhaps the episode would be clearer if he were on stage earlier observing Monticelso and Lodovico's interview, echoing the many other scenes in the play where characters are secretly observed.

Act V scene 1

The scene shifts to Bracciano's palace in Padua, where his and Vittoria's wedding celebrations are taking place. Flamineo talks with Hortensio, a member of Bracciano's household, about the Moor who has recently arrived with his companions, two Hungarian noblemen who have entered the order of Capuchin monks. Bracciano welcomes the Moor, Mulinassar, who has offered him his service in the likely war against Francisco de Medici. He invites the visitors to attend a duelling competition as part of the celebrations, which is also to be attended by the foreign ambassadors, en route from the papal election in Rome to their native countries. Left alone, the visitors are revealed to be Francisco, disguised as the

Moor, Lodovico and Gasparo as the Capuchins, and Antonelli also in disguise. They are greeted by Carlo and Pedro, members of Bracciano's household who are secretly in league with Francisco. Their discussion of their impending revenge on Bracciano is interrupted by Flamineo, Marcello and Zanche. The disguised Francisco talks with Flamineo and Marcello before going off to watch the duelling. Then Hortensio questions Flamineo about his relationship with Zanche, who knows about his villainy, and to whom he has promised marriage. A brief exchange of wit between Flamineo and Zanche is cut short when Cornelia appears and strikes her, and Marcello kicks her, resulting in an argument between him and Flamineo, culminating in threats and challenges. The disguised Francisco returns and Zanche, left alone with him, expresses her love for him as her supposed countryman. Francisco rejects her, but muses to himself that she may be useful to him.

The phrase, 'The plot thickens', might have been devised for this scene. The start of Act V does seem rather late in the play for such a plethora of plot twists: the wedding celebrations of Bracciano and Vittoria; Francisco in his totally unanticipated Moorish disguise, with Lodovico and Gasparo as his supporting Hungarian Capuchins; the revelation of a hitherto unexpected relationship between Flamineo and Zanche, and her subsequent attraction to the visiting Moor; the challenge that suddenly erupts between Flamineo and Marcello; not to mention a number of new, minor characters: Hortensio, Carlo, Pedro and a young lord. The scene's variety is matched by an equally varied selection of modes of discourse, from Flamineo's unadorned, informative, matter-of-fact account of the Moor and his companions, in both verse and prose (lines 5–27) to the same character's characteristic tone of cynical mockery, crammed with figurative flourishes and unpleasant imagery and also veering between verse and prose, with which he recounts his relationship with Zanche (lines 152–85). Bracciano, confident in his newly married state and apparently secure in his own palace, greets his Moorish guest in formal, stately verse (lines 44–62). With rather pompous assurance, he gloats over the fact that the foreign ambassadors have deigned to grace his wedding celebrations, despite his and Vittoria's excommunication by the new Pope — something of a political triumph for him.

The language of the disguised Francisco is particularly worthy of note: 'Mulinassar' is a prose character, fitting his down-to-earth, soldierly persona. He affects a blunt, no-nonsense modesty, refusing to 'wash [his] mouth with [his] own praise', while also declining to 'flatter' his host. Webster gives him a number of observations on the unfairness of the social class structure, presenting him almost in the role of a malcontent. He suggests that differences in social status are a sham, depending on 'mere chance' just as much as the positioning of a brick 'on the top of a turret' as opposed to 'the bottom of a well'. He also attacks the hypocrisy of outward appearances, asserting that courtiers who 'seem Colossuses in a chamber' would appear 'pitiful pigmies' on a battlefield. Webster is playing with our responses here. Perhaps we agree with these statements apparently promoting social equality, yet we should not forget that they are spoken by someone equally guilty

of presenting a false appearance as those he attacks; one who, moreover, is in reality a powerful duke. Various levels of irony are thus at work in the portrayal of the disguised Francisco, and his visual appearance, in dark-skinned make-up, casts a different light on the play's title.

This, in turn, alerts a modern audience or reader to the cultural attitudes to racial difference prevalent in the early seventeenth century. Even then London was a cosmopolitan city, with many non-white immigrants and visitors. The 6-month visit of the King of Barbary's ambassador and his retinue to the court of Queen Elizabeth caused particular excitement in 1600. Moors were represented in a number of plays of the period, including three contrasting portrayals in Shakespeare: Aaron, the ruthless machiavellian villain in *Titus Andronicus*; the Prince of Morocco, Portia's comically bombastic suitor in *The Merchant of Venice*; and the tragic hero of *Othello*, transformed by jealousy from nobility to bestiality. Even in these three examples, evidence of what we would call racist assumptions in the way the characters are presented is complex and contradictory, but there can be little doubt that, for most people in Elizabethan and Jacobean England, the white-skinned races of northern Europe were inherently superior to other racial types. Dark-complexioned women were deemed less attractive than those with fair skin, and the issue is morally problematised by the association of whiteness with virtue and blackness with evil. In many respects our civilisation has not advanced much, and it is salutary to remember that, even though black actors had played Othello since the eighteenth century, white actors were still blacking up for the role as late as the 1980s, before such a practice became ideologically unacceptable. With the role of Francisco, of course, there is no avoiding such a potentially offensive representation since, as Mulinassar, he is a white man disguised by dark make-up and ethnic costuming. Fortunately for modern sensibilities, Webster has presented 'Mulinassar' as a character of dignity and principle, whose statements of social equality may be taken to apply just as much to racial identity. When he asks, 'what difference is between the duke and I?', we may, in fact, be more likely today to assume he is commenting on their differences in race and arguing for their common humanity.

The issue is less clear-cut in relation to Zanche, and there are conflicting signals in Webster's presentation of her, given an extra dimension of discrepant awareness in early performances through the role's being played by a white, boy actor. Zanche shows a limited awareness of her racial standing in Italian society. She is obviously excited to see her 'countryman, a goodly person' visiting Padua, and relishes the prospect of conversation with him 'in our own language' — a potentially complicating factor that Webster apparently abandons, since it would doubtless have tested Francisco's linguistic skill! In expressing her attraction to 'Mulinassar' she confesses, 'I ne'er loved my complexion till now', a comment that suggests she has always been made conscious of her inferior status in white society. Otherwise, Webster stresses Zanche's sexual predilections rather than her race through her role in this scene.

Other characters, though, seem more concerned with her racial status. In an implicit comment on her blackness, Marcello and Flamineo classify her as a 'devil' in lines 86–91, an image Flamineo extends in his later conversation with Hortensio (lines 151–66): she is a 'witch' and a 'gipsy' who has elicited a 'dark promise' of marriage from him. Though Flamineo's language towards her is as much misogynistic as it is racist, he reveals his underlying prejudice in his reference to Mulinassar as 'your sunburnt gentleman'. Such attitudes may well reflect those common at the time; however, it is important to remember they are largely expressed through the character of Flamineo, whose moral attitudes are not exactly endorsed by the play.

Act V scene 2

As Marcello denies to Cornelia that he is engaged to fight a duel, Flamineo enters and runs him through with his own sword. Cornelia will not accept at first that Marcello is dead, shies away from stabbing Flamineo, and gives a false account to Bracciano, claiming that the incident was Marcello's fault. Bracciano orders that Vittoria should not be told what has happened, and Flamineo is allowed to remain alive on a day-by-day basis. Bracciano, who is armed for the duelling contest, calls for his helmet, which the disguised Lodovico has sprinkled with poison.

Key developments from the previous scene quickly unfold in this short, dramatic episode. Time enough has passed for Cornelia to have heard rumours that Marcello is to fight a duel, and the scene centres on her. As befits her moral virtue, established in Act I scene 2, her language here associates her with a simple Christian piety. Images of blessing, prayer, heaven and repentance are constantly on her lips, together with references to God; and the crucifix which is a key emblem of the scene is presumably the one she is wearing round her neck. Though the crucifix, broken by the baby Flamineo as he took the milk from his mother's breast, has since been mended, nothing can repair either Marcello, the 'limb' of the family cut off by his brother, or Cornelia's shattered mind. She responds to what has happened by a process of emotional denial, first that Marcello is indeed dead, and then that his death is Flamineo's fault. Despite Flamineo's guilt, and despite her initial instinct to avenge Marcello's death by stabbing him, she ends determined that having lost one son she will not lose another. She concludes her spoken role in the scene with a rhyming couplet that seals the audience's sympathy for her grief and anguish.

Cornelia does not have a monopoly on moral values in this scene — nor is she the only character who lies or prevaricates. Indeed, as in her case, most of the other characters demonstrate contradictory moral behaviour. Marcello, for the best of motives perhaps, emphatically denies that he is engaged to fight a duel. ''Tis not so', he affirms, but almost immediately his words are proved false. Dying, he proclaims himself punished for the sins of his family, who have 'rise[n] / By all dishonest means'. Though Hortensio reaffirms Marcello's moral status (he was 'good Marcello' at II.1.366; now he is 'Virtuous Marcello'), our response is more ambivalent on account of his intemperate behaviour in the previous scene. Even so, it is a shock when his own mother attempts to unload on him the responsibility for his own death.

Flamineo's behaviour, too, is difficult to assess. His violent assault on his brother, against all the laws of duelling, is shocking. However, he promises to send a surgeon — who never appears — and, instead of taking sanctuary as he says he will, he returns with Bracciano, admits what he has done, calling it his 'misfortune', and meekly accepts his punishment: 'Your will is law now, I'll not meddle with it'. In itself, this punishment also demonstrates Bracciano's moral prevarication. He takes control of the situation, offers comfort to his mother-in-law, is solicitous for the feelings of his wife and apparently withholds his pardon from Flamineo. His sentence, though, virtually amounts to a pardon, as Francisco notes at the end of the scene; yet it also asserts his daily control over Flamineo, in revenge for Flamineo's 'brav[ing]' of him earlier in the play (see IV.2.42–71). Thus, in apparently meting out both justice and mercy, he is in reality consolidating his own position and getting back at his brother-in-law.

Francisco's closing speech, his only verbal contribution to the scene, exemplifies the moral ambivalence that attaches to virtually all of the characters in the play. As an aside, we assume the speech to represent his true feelings; consequently we are given a disturbing picture of a man adhering to mutually exclusive moral positions. He expresses pity for Bracciano's impending death while rejoicing in his imminent passage to hell; and he castigates Bracciano's pardoning of a murderer while he himself is about to become one (his reference to the pardon as a 'good deed' is clearly ironic). The moral world of the play is thus confirmed as one where human beings can be simultaneously virtuous and wicked, apparently unaware of the contradictions they embody.

As Bracciano leaves for his participation in the barriers with his poisoned helmet, Webster racks up the tension almost unbearably. In passing, we might also note that the dramatist has manipulated time in the scene: while the imminence of the duelling contest suggests no time gap since the previous scene, we are also required to accept that enough time has passed for rumours of Flamineo and Marcello's impending duel to have spread throughout the court. Such temporal duality is very common in plays of the period, and generally goes unnoticed in the theatre.

Act V scene 3

After the duelling contest, Bracciano suffers the effects of the poisoned helmet. He sends his armourer off to be tortured, but tells the distressed Vittoria that Francisco is responsible. Lodovico and Gasparo, in their Capuchin disguise, take him to his room to administer the last rites, but he is shortly brought back in his bed, raving and distracted. He is left alone with the supposed Capuchins, who reveal their true identity and strangle him. Vittoria is distraught at his death but, in conversation with the disguised Francisco, Flamineo is sceptical of her grief. Zanche reveals to 'Mulinassar' the true circumstances of Camillo and Isabella's deaths, tells him she plans to rob Vittoria, and arranges to meet him at midnight to run away together. Francisco and Lodovico reflect on the justification for their actions.

There are many surprises in this scene, but perhaps its most surprising feature is Vittoria's limited role in it. Apart from her fleeting appearance in the wedding procession at the start of Act V scene 1, we have not seen her since Act IV scene 2 — a long absence for someone who is ostensibly the play's title character. In this scene, she is restricted to eight utterances, expressing her distress for Bracciano ('O my loved lord! Poisoned?'; 'O my good lord!') and her own anguish ('I am lost for ever'; 'O me! This place is hell'). An actor in the role will need to sustain the emotional force of these responses whenever Vittoria is on stage, and her visible presence, together with the physical expressions of her emotional state, will give her more prominence in the theatre than she seems to have in the text. However, the lack of any extended outpouring of grief or anger is an interesting textual 'absence'.

The focus of the scene is Bracciano's death, which Webster draws out, at unnecessary length, through three distinct stages. First, there is his entrance suffering from the effects of the poisoned helmet; this section concludes as he retreats to his 'cabinet' accompanied by the supposed Capuchins ready to give him 'extreme unction'. An audience will probably assume that this will be his last appearance, and that his offstage death will shortly be announced. Webster, however, has other plans, and brings Bracciano back in his bed for an extended and somewhat gratuitous mad scene, his utterances veering from nonsense to satirical sense, reflecting the idea of 'Reason in madness' developed in Shakespeare's *King Lear* (*The Tragedy of King Lear*, IV.5.171). Finally, his lingering death is concluded by the gloating ministrations of the 'Capuchins', as Lodovico and Gasparo reveal their true identities and deliver the *coup de grâce* by strangling him. The whole of this sequence has a distinctly Gothic quality and, in typical Jacobean fashion, it is imbued with undercurrents of comedy that occasionally threaten to break to the surface. Notably, Bracciano's misogynistic observation, 'How miserable a thing it is to die /'Mongst women howling!' has an incongruous comic effect, and his sudden recovery of his wits just as Lodovico and Gasparo are about to strangle him is an openly comic moment: 'O the cursèd devil, /Come to himself again! We are undone'; as Lodovico later admits, their intention of terrifying him 'at the last gasp' recoiled on them so that 'the duke had like /T'have terrified us'.

Comedy of a different kind is developed in Bracciano's distracted babblings. At first he is driven to bitter observations on life and the futility of worldly power. He reflects on the ingratitude of 'great men's [...] friends' in times of need, a situation explored in Shakespeare's *Timon of Athens*; and on his inability to lengthen his own life despite having had the power of life and death over 'offending slaves /And wretched murderers' — perhaps referring to his recent pardoning of Flamineo. He regrets not experiencing the peacefulness of 'soft natural death', suffering instead the 'horror [that] waits on princes'. When he is brought back on stage in his bed, however, such observations are couched in grotesque humour. It is interesting that Webster obviously wants to make clear to the reader of the text that these speeches are to be regarded as '*several kinds of distractions*', thus diverting attention from their more serious satirical content, in which

Bracciano attacks financial irregularities of various kinds (see lines 84–87, 107–09), culminating in a vision of Flamineo 'dancing on the ropes' with a 'money-bag in each hand, to keep him even'. Is Bracciano explicitly condemning the bribery and corruption practised by his secretary? Flamineo perhaps thinks so, commenting, 'I do not like that he names me so often, / Especially on's death-bed'. Bracciano also attacks lawyers and churchmen; rails against Francisco, 'That old dog-fox, that politician Florence'; has visions of the devil; and indulges in a vividly eccentric description of Vittoria, with her powdered hair, looking as if she has 'sinned in the pastry' (i.e. the part of the kitchen where pastry is made) and is covered in flour. Such combinations of sense and nonsense, with their comic tone, are typical of mad scenes in Elizabethan and Jacobean drama.

Bracciano's most important lines in the scene, however, are spoken before his distraction takes hold of him, and express his feelings for Vittoria:

> Where's this good woman? Had I infinite worlds
> They were too little for thee. Must I leave thee?

Though 'good woman' seems a hardly adequate description of Vittoria, Bracciano's expression of adoration for her seems genuine, and it is her name that springs to his lips when he briefly recovers his wits in the face of Lodovico and Gasparo's taunts, becoming his final utterance in the play. Yet in view of their previous stormy relationship, we are still led to question the nature of their feelings towards each other, a questioning which is channelled in this scene principally through Flamineo.

Twice in the scene, Flamineo engages in conversation with the disguised Francisco, on both occasions offering typical examples of his malcontent's philosophy. In particular, he notes cynically how flatterers fall away from 'dying princes' (see lines 42–47) and how great men end up being 'censured by their slaves', both for their bad deeds and their failure to fulfil all men's wishes (see lines 202–05). Appropriately, Flamineo demonstrates the truth of his observations by himself giving vent to critical comments about Bracciano, as well as about Vittoria. He suggests that those who now mourn for Bracciano 'do but weep over their stepmothers' graves', in other words their tears are insincere; and goes on to say that he himself would have cheated his master if he had had 'cunning enough'. In response to Francisco's request that he should 'speak freely' what he really thought of him, he characterises Bracciano as being more concerned with his finances than with the lives of his subjects, and concludes that 'to over-commend some [princes] is palpable lying'. Turning his attention to Vittoria, he condemns her for the insincerity of her grief, which he sums up with a typically misogynistic observation, 'There's nothing sooner dry than women's tears'. It is difficult to know how we should respond to Flamineo's attacks on his sister and brother-in-law. Are these his genuine feelings, or is he merely trotting out the bitterly cynical views expected of a malcontent, for the benefit of the disguised Francisco? Perhaps he is still indulging in the feigned 'mad humour' he adopted earlier in the play (see III.2.304–07).

Equally ambiguous is Flamineo's exit from the scene, which again could represent genuine or feigned emotion. He is suddenly taken with an urge to speak to the dead Bracciano, determining to do so 'though forty devils / Wait on him in his livery of flames'; and he exits intending to 'shake him by the hand' whatever the consequences. Here, as in the whole scene, the actor playing Flamineo will need to decide where the borderline lies between the character's outward appearance and inner reality, though for the audience his ambiguity will almost certainly remain.

The intrigue between Zanche and Francisco that closes the scene seems almost redundant, serving principally to confirm Francisco and Lodovico in their revenge by revealing to them the exact circumstances of Isabella and Camillo's deaths. It is a conscious effort for the reader to keep in mind Francisco's disguise as Mulinassar, particularly as Webster does not sustain the distinctive prose style originally established for the feigned Moor; in this respect, theatre audiences have the visual dimension of the disguise constantly before them (the same applies, of course, to Lodovico and Gasparo). The actor playing Francisco will also, presumably, alter his voice as appropriate. The scene with Zanche is punctuated by Lodovico's sardonic comments, some of which, though not marked as such in the text, are presumably spoken aside to Francisco in Lodovico's own voice. Lodovico takes Zanche's revelations as justification for their actions, but Francisco is contemptuous of such a response: 'Tush for justice'. For him, the 'fame' of their 'enterprise' — in other words the honourable reputation it will give them — is sufficient to cleanse any shame attached to their methods.

Webster's portrayal of Zanche is worth a note here. To Francisco and Lodovico she is 'infernal' — a reference to her dark skin which, in the culture of the period, links her with hell and devils. She herself is perhaps referring to such associations when she notes her own part in the 'black deed' of the murders, later claiming that the money she intends to steal from Vittoria will provide a dowry for her intended marriage to 'Mulinassar' that will wash them both white. In this statement, not only do we see the underlying cultural assumption of the superiority of whiteness, but also an indication of the power of money, which can raise social position in the face of racial 'inferiority'. We should also be aware that Mulinassar's dark skin can indeed be washed white, while Zanche's use of language arouses complex and ironic echoes of the play's title.

Like Flamineo, Zanche recognises the insincerity of the 'court tears' shed for Bracciano, but she is more concerned with her designs on Mulinassar — recounting her 'sad dream' (which he turns into a parallel dream of explicit sexual activity), revealing the truth about Isabella and Camillo's deaths, and promising to share with him the money she intends to steal from Vittoria. Her feelings for her 'countryman' (V.1.94) amount almost to an obsession, which can be played for either its serious intensity or its comic effect. Having established the arrangements of her 'flight' with the supposed Moor, she leaves, but returns almost immediately to confirm their midnight assignation in the chapel. This re-entry is potentially comic in two ways: it reveals Zanche's over-eager anxiety, and it takes Francisco and Lodovico by surprise, almost catching them out as they relax into their real selves.

Act V scene 4

Giovanni has succeeded to the dukedom. Flamineo criticises him behind his back but is civil to his face; however, Giovanni sends word that Flamineo is not to come near him. Francisco, still disguised as Mulinassar, reports on Cornelia's grief for Marcello. Cornelia is then revealed, with Zanche and other ladies, wrapping Marcello's corpse in its winding-sheet; she is crazed with grief, which arouses Flamineo's compassion. Left alone, he is haunted by Bracciano's ghost, which seems to foretell his death. He goes off to confront Vittoria.

Cornelia's madness and Bracciano's ghost combine to form another potent Gothic mix, set against the dignity and authority of the young Giovanni. Centrally, though, the scene is about Flamineo, exploring the apparent awakening in him of 'compassion' and 'conscience'. His killing of his brother, Marcello, now determines other characters' reactions to him, and Francisco has apparently not revealed Flamineo's part in Camillo's murder. As elsewhere, Flamineo's language combines verse and prose, subtly delineating shifts in his role and status. Here, his cynical speeches in the first part of the scene, including his disparaging and then his false flattery of Giovanni, are largely in prose, while his final speech, including his response to Bracciano's ghost and his tortured self-analysis, amount to a powerful blank-verse soliloquy. At this stage in the play, it would be reasonable to argue that Flamineo is in fact the main character.

Flamineo's verbal attacks on Giovanni — 'behind him' rather than 'to his face' — are motivated largely by the potential threat the new young duke poses to him, with his eagle's talons ('tallants') that will 'grow out in time'. His fears are almost instantly proved true; not only does Giovanni advise him to 'Study [his] prayers' and 'be penitent', but banishes him from his own immediate vicinity. Flamineo's emotional disintegration is already apparent at this stage of the scene: 'I am falling to pieces already', he admits. His resentment at his treatment emerges in unfocused threats: 'I'll smoor [suffocate] some of them'; and it is clearly his loss of the social position he has worked so hard to establish that rankles. He refers to himself as 'a pitiful /Degraded courtier' and later determines to find out 'what my rich sister means /T'assign me for my service'. Clearly he remains as obsessed with his social and financial status as he was at the start of the play.

Though he refers contemptuously to the grief of Cornelia and her ladies as 'superstitious howling', it is clear that the spectacle of his mother's madness as she wraps Marcello in his shroud has a profound effect on Flamineo. As Cornelia inspects his hand for the signs of his guilt, he wishes himself somewhere else: 'I would I were from hence'. The stirrings of his compassion, a feeling hitherto alien to him, are powerfully expressed in his lines on Cornelia's exit, and his request for Mulinassar to leave him indicates a shift towards introspection in his character. Recognising that he has lived 'riotously ill', he claims to have sometimes felt 'the maze of conscience', and asserts that this night will determine his fate.

The appearance of Bracciano's ghost, like that of Isabella earlier in the play, could be read as a figment of Flamineo's imagination revealing his innermost anxieties, though

he himself denies such an interpretation, claiming, 'This is beyond melancholy'. In dramatic terms the ghost is an effective and sinister device that serves a largely emblematic function. The leather cassock, a long military coat or cloak, was traditionally worn by ghosts in tragedies, while the cowl, a monk's hooded robe, was often used as a male burial garment, in the hope that the dead man would be granted remission of his sins. The skull and the earth are obvious symbols of death, as is the lily, though this also carries other associations, of lust and of false appearance — a beautiful flower with a foul smell. Webster's contemporary audience would be skilled in interpreting visual emblems, detecting multiple layers of meaning that are likely to pass their modern counterparts by. The ghost does not need to speak to answer Flamineo's questions; its very appearance and actions would be enough to affirm that Bracciano's spirit is in the 'cursèd dungeon' of hell rather than in heaven's 'starry gallery', punished for his crimes of murder and lechery; and that Flamineo is destined soon to join him in death. Despite the 'horrors' he has experienced in this scene, which he enumerates in lines 147–50, Flamineo remains defiant: 'I do dare my fate / To do its worst'. He clings on to the thought of 'bounty' or generosity from his 'rich sister'; if she fails him in this respect, he threatens to kill her. Flamineo's is a powerful role in this scene, offering tremendous opportunities for an actor to extend the character's emotional range and depth.

Cornelia's madness requires some comment. It is a conventionally stylised portrayal of mental distraction, with its combination of sense and nonsense, its snatches of song and rhyme, and the giving out of real or imaginary herbs and flowers. Specifically, it owes a great deal to the madness of Ophelia in *Hamlet*, and the effect should be similarly touching, awkward, painful, embarrassing and moving, rather than caricatured and shrill, as it can be in performance. A visual dimension likely to be missed in a mere reading of the text is the image of Cornelia and the ladies '*winding* MARCELLO's *cor[p]se*'. Revealed as a tableau as Flamineo draws aside the traverse curtain, this is suggestive of a *pietà*, a representation of the Virgin Mary tending Christ's body after its removal from the cross. Such an image again associates Cornelia and Marcello with moral virtue, but perhaps carries a hint of irony in this context. Its effect on an audience can be manipulated by the way the onstage characters are shown to react when the tableau is revealed.

Act V scene 5

Lodovico urges Francisco to leave Padua and rely on him to complete their revenge. Overhearing their conversation, Hortensio decides to call up armed opposition.

This short scene gives a sense of events nearing their conclusion, and marks yet another instance of characters being overheard by onstage eavesdroppers. Lodovico exhibits unexpected concern for Francisco — for his reputation, perhaps, as much as for his personal safety. It is not clear whose 'murder' is being discussed, but we are likely to assume that Flamineo and/or Vittoria are the intended victims. Exaggerating,

perhaps, Lodovico promises to exact vengeance on 'all in this bold assembly' including 'the meanest follower'. What is notable is how Francisco still ennobles the act of revenge as a 'glorious act' bringing everlasting 'fame' to the perpetrators. Francisco's observation that Lodovico may 'perish' in their project, together with Hortensio's resolution to 'raise some force' in opposition to them, creates a sense of considerable tension in the audience's anticipation of the play's outcome.

Act V scene 6

Flamineo demands his reward from Vittoria for his services to her; when she offers only her curse, he returns with two pairs of pistols, claiming he had sworn to Bracciano that neither he nor Vittoria should outlive him longer than 4 hours. Zanche persuades Vittoria to humour Flamineo by persuading him to die first. They shoot him using one pair of pistols, having sworn then to turn the other pair on each other; however, he has tricked them by loading the pistols with powder but no shot. As they triumph over him, he rises from his apparent death throes, rebukes them for their treachery and threatens them with the second pair of pistols. He is fore-stalled, though, when Lodovico and the other conspirators burst in, throw off their disguises and declare their intention of avenging Isabella's murder. They kill Vittoria, Flamineo and Zanche before armed guards break into the room with Giovanni and the foreign ambassadors. Lodovico is shot and wounded, and Giovanni sends him and the other conspirators to be imprisoned and tortured.

Webster has provided an explosive conclusion to *The White Devil*, with complex twists and turns of plot and character, final reflections on the main themes of the play, an unex-pectedly comic interlude, and a range of brilliant and impressive poetic flourishes. This commentary can only deal briefly with selected aspects of the scene.

Perhaps the most surprising element is Flamineo's fake death. There is something inherently comic in the way Vittoria and Zanche double-cross Flamineo to save their own skins, though how far it is played as comedy depends on the actors and director. But when the apparently dying Flamineo pops up again, unharmed, presumably with a huge grin on his face, there is no escaping Webster's comic purpose. The question is, why does he do this at this stage in the play? One effect is precisely what Flamineo says: 'to prove [the women's] kindness' to him, and it is a test they comprehensively fail, showing Vittoria, particularly, at her worst. Perhaps Webster is aware, too, of how the killings at the ends of tragedies can arouse laughter in the audience and therefore provides a comic release before the tragic denouement.

Another odd feature of the scene, by modern standards, is the way Webster uses it almost as a debating chamber for ideas such as courtly power and corruption, and the nature of women, that have been central to the play. Many of the statements made by the characters on these issues are couched in the form of Webster's characteristic *sententiae*, sometimes highlighted by the use of rhyming couplets.

Appropriately, in view of his status as malcontent, it is Flamineo who is given many of the observations about the fickleness and injustice of court patronage. Echoing Lodovico's cynical jibe at 'Courtly reward, / And punishment' in Act I scene 1, he demands from Vittoria the 'Reward for [his] long service' and comments bitterly, 'My life hath done service to other men'. What that service entails is made clear in his dying speech, where he advises 'all that belong to great men' to beware of the sunshine of their favours, which will inevitably be followed by the 'winter' of their ingratitude. 'Belong' is a revealing choice of verb, suggesting as it does that great men's servants, like Flamineo himself, are no more than chattels or possessions. It is Vittoria, though, who crystallises the perils of courtly life in her generalised but memorable couplet:

> O happy they that never saw the court,
> Nor ever knew great man but by report.

This is an axiom that applies to great men themselves, as well as to their followers, as Flamineo points out in noting that, 'If he [Bracciano] could not be safe in his own court / Being a great duke, what hope then for us?'

Some characters in the play find an alternative to social subservience in asserting their own individuality or selfhood. This is what has motivated Flamineo throughout the play, and it is made more explicit in this scene. 'I would not live at any man's entreaty / Nor die at any's bidding', he declares, concluding: 'My death shall serve mine own turn'. Though these comments are offered in the face of the 'fake' death he is facing, they are maintained when real death beckons, as he affirms, 'at myself I will begin and end'. This existentialist philosophy is shared by Lodovico, who states it explicitly at the end of the scene: 'I do glory yet / That I can call this act mine own'. Such relish of his own selfhood is then given alternative expression in a metaphor of artistic creativity, suggesting that the bloody revenge he has enacted is like a masterpiece in the genre of painting depicting night-time scenes: 'I limbed [painted] this night-piece and it was my best'. Though he is facing 'The rack, the gallows, and the torturing wheel', there is no mistaking his sense of triumph in what he has achieved.

Flamineo's expression of his individuality is actually borrowed from Vittoria in the trial scene, when she says, 'I scorn to hold my life / At yours or any man's entreaty, sir'. On her tongue, however, there is a strong implication of gender in the use of the word 'man', so that she is asserting not just her selfhood but her womanhood. Vittoria is a strong-willed woman in a man's world — a world, moreover, in which male attitudes to women are habitually misogynistic. Such misogyny is constantly on Flamineo's lips in this scene. When Vittoria pleads passionately for her life, he dismisses her words as mere 'grammatical laments, / Feminine arguments' which lack 'sense / Of reason, or sound doctrine'. The implication is that women's intellect is by definition superficial and irrational. When the women double-cross him and shoot him, he refers to them contemptuously as 'braches' or bitches before revealing the trick he has played on them and launching into an extended attack on female betrayal and wickedness. He talks of the hypocrisy of grieving wives who almost immediately remarry, echoing the disgust felt by Shakespeare's Hamlet at his mother's behaviour, and sums up bitterly, 'Trust a woman? — Never, never'. Applying a classical allusion to illustrate his attack on the faithlessness of married women, he chooses the tale of Hypermnestra, the only one out of 50 sisters to spare her husband's life — conveniently forgetting that the slaughter was committed at the behest of their father.

The revengeful Lodovico shares something of Flamineo's misogyny, reflecting the court's attitude to Vittoria earlier in the play. Again, she is a 'glorious strumpet' who has been 'a most prodigious comet'. The language of both phrases suggests a kind of splendid display in Vittoria's behaviour, the very opposite of the modesty seen as appropriate to women. 'Prodigious' suggests that such 'unfeminine' behaviour is an inevitable precursor to disaster. A prodigy is an extraordinary phenomenon such as an eclipse, an earthquake or, indeed, a comet, that was usually interpreted as a sign of dire events to come.

Vittoria's courage in the face of death, though, is shown in a positive light, and she herself interprets this quality as more truly feminine, showing her as 'too true a woman'. Zanche echoes her courage, and in her case it becomes a triumphant assertion of her race as much as her gender: 'I am proud /Death cannot alter my complexion, /For I shall ne'er look pale'. The women's resolution is impressive enough to redirect Flamineo's misogyny, though his comments about 'women that are famed / For masculine virtue' remain ambiguous. However, he finds a new admiration for Vittoria — 'Th'art a noble sister — /I love thee now' — and suggests that 'if woman do breed man /She ought to teach him manhood'. These sentiments would have aroused mixed feelings in Webster's original audiences, challenging as they do some of the traditional assumptions about women's role in society. In evoking such an ambivalent response to Vittoria throughout the play, eliciting admiration for qualities not generally encouraged in women, Webster stirs debate about controversial issues — a characteristic feature of Jacobean drama.

In terms of its vocabulary, the final scene revisits most of the play's central imagery, often couched in richly metaphorical language. Devils and diseases, beasts and jewels, black and white, light and darkness, heaven and hell and the insidious dangers of false appearance all continue to influence the ideas and atmosphere of the play in its final stages. Particularly striking is the way Webster fills the scene with images of violence and death. Words such as 'die', 'dying', 'death', 'deadly', 'live', 'life', 'outlive', 'kill', 'killed', 'blood', 'bloody', 'bleed', 'violent', 'violence', 'murderer', 'graves', 'sacrifice', 'worm', 'winding-sheet' and 'epitaphs' pervade the scene, accompanied by a variety of related atmospheric vocabulary such as 'horror', 'horrid', 'haunted', 'ominous', 'despair', 'pain' and 'punishment'. The ending of the play is steeped in death, but the nature of death is as vague and elusive as the meaning of life, and when Flamineo exclaims 'O, I am in a mist', he could be referring to either.

The conclusion of the play is unusual, ending as it does with a child taking control and granted the authority of the final lines. The visual contrast between the young duke and the grizzled murderer and pirate, Lodovico, is particularly telling, suggesting a new

generation that will promote the demands of 'justice' in the sight of 'heaven' without fear or favour. Gone is Giovanni's childish obsession with militarism, to be replaced by the idealism of a moral crusader against 'black deeds' committed by 'bloody villains'. If Lodovico has anticipated approval of the revenge he has exacted on the prince's behalf, backed by his uncle Francisco, he is in for a shock, which an actor can register powerfully on stage. Giovanni's outrage at his uncle's behaviour — 'He turned murderer?' — and his swift condemnation of the villains 'to prison, and to torture' suggests a new zero-tolerance regime, with his final couplet powerfully emphasising the fragility of evil. The impact of this ending can vary in performance, of course, and partly depends on the age of the boy cast as Giovanni. If he is particularly young — under 10, say — surrounded by adults, his authority might be made to look either particularly impressive or particularly delicate. It is worth noting here the use Webster makes of the foreign ambassadors, especially the English one, who acts as protector to the young duke and orders the guards to fire on the murderers: 'Keep back the prince. — Shoot, shoot!' It is presumably him Giovanni addresses at the end as 'my honoured lord', apparently investing in him the responsibility for the villains' 'punishment'. At key moments this character has, in few words, guided the audience's response, and the play's violent Italianate society has been viewed as if through the prism of foreign observance. Again, there is ambiguity here. For some, the English ambassador would doubtless have seemed like a reassuring representative of British common sense and moral superiority. For others, the play's Italian setting would have appeared as a thinly-disguised representation of the political and moral corruption endemic in all societies, including England.

Characters and characterisation

One of the most common errors made by students is to write about characters in literature as if they were real people. In reality, they are linguistic constructs created to fulfil a range of purposes in different texts. While an assessment of the 'personality' of a fictional or dramatic character may be a valid part of literary analysis, it is much more relevant to examine characterisation — the techniques a writer uses to create particular characters for particular purposes. When it comes to a play, the 'text' belonging to each character is a blueprint for interpretation by different actors, and one important aspect of analysis is to consider the range of potential performances that a text makes available.

Modern readers and audiences often look for psychological consistency in the portrayal of character, but this concept would have been alien to Webster and his contemporaries. Characters function at each moment in a play script according to the dramatic needs of that moment, and while there may often be a clear sense of consistency or development, characters in Jacobean drama are equally often contra-dictory and ambiguous. An illusion of coherence can be created in performance by the fact that a single actor is playing the role, and the overall effect is often to suggest the inconsistency and complexity of real people.

Characters in a play are defined through language and action. What they do, what they say, how they say it, and what other characters say about them determine the response of a reader, while on stage these techniques of characterisation are enhanced by costume, gesture, facial expression and other performance features. In examining the text, you need to be sensitive to the characters' use of verse or prose, the rhetorical and figurative qualities of their speech, the imagery they use and that associated with them, and the tone of their language. Characters who are given soliloquies are placed in a privileged position in relation to members of the audience, who are allowed to share their innermost thoughts.

These notes offer some general pointers to approaching the characters in *The White Devil*; a more detailed response has already been offered in the scene summaries and commentary section (pages 22–60), which you should use in conjunction with this section. As the relationships between the characters are particularly complex in this play, the following chart may help you to keep track of who's who:

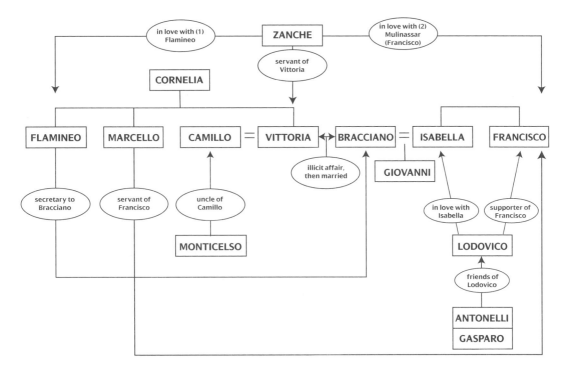

Vittoria

Often regarded as the play's title character, Vittoria in fact has surprisingly few scenes, and offers an enigmatic presence at the heart of the play. The undoubted impact she makes on an audience is created in just four scenes: her two encounters with Bracciano (I.2 and IV.2); her trial (III.2); and her death scene (V.6). She appears only as a silent member of the wedding procession that opens V.1 and says little during Bracciano's death scene (V.3), yet we carry away from the play a powerful if ambiguous sense of her as the 'glorious strumpet' and 'prodigious comet' of Lodovico's half-admiring condemnation (V.6.206, 214). She is a brilliant, attractive, impressive figure whose dignified but emotional self-defence at her trial for adultery more-or-less blinds us to her complicity in murder. In the face of death, she demonstrates a defiant courage: in demanding the right to be killed before her servant; in refusing to shrink from the weapons drawn against her; in denying her killers the spectacle of her tears; and in asserting her womanhood (see V.6.216–26). At the end, however, she also attains something of the fearful self-knowledge and social awareness that attaches to the heroes and heroines of tragedy, confessing that she is being punished for the 'sin' that 'lay in [her] blood' (V.6.240–41); greeting the 'black storm' of her end with trepidation (V.6.248–49); and bemoaning her association with 'the court' and its 'great [men]', blaming these for her downfall (V.6.261–62). The audience's response to her throughout this sequence is partly conditioned by that of Flamineo, who shifts from contempt for her treachery to admiration of her 'masculine virtue' (V.6.245).

In the light of this, it is easy to forget Vittoria's many faults, which in another context might have justified regarding her as a wicked, manipulative villain. There can be little doubt that her account of her 'foolish idle dream' (I.2.232) is specifically intended to encourage Bracciano into plotting the murders of Isabella and Camillo. Her self-defence at her trial is disingenuous to say the least, impressing us not because of her innocence but because of her spirited attack on the self-evident hypocrisy of her accusers. Her attack on Bracciano as the architect of her shame, though justified by his mistaken accusations of faithlessness, is similarly based on a twisting of the truth. Her vindictive triumphing over Flamineo when she thinks she has turned his own trap against him merely makes her into the same 'cursèd devil' as she accuses him of being (V.6.123), and the sight of her and Zanche '*tread[ing] upon him*' (V.6.118SD) is far from edifying.

Ultimately, then, Vittoria demonstrates the play's double vision of humanity, its philosophical exploration of evil masquerading as virtue and beauty. As such, she certainly exemplifies the oxymoron of the title, though she is far from being the only character to do so.

Flamineo

Flamineo's role is the largest in the play, featuring in 12 of its 16 scenes, including the dumbshow. However, it seems inappropriate to regard him as the play's protagonist; perhaps it is his own sense of his depressed status, together with his essentially manipulative role, that makes him seem secondary to Vittoria and Bracciano. A lot depends, however, on what an actor brings to the part, and it is possible that it was just as much of a star role for Richard Perkins in 1612 as it was for Richard McCabe in the RSC's 1996 production.

Flamineo remains essentially manipulative from beginning to end of the play. Whether he is manoeuvring Camillo out of the way to facilitate a meeting between Bracciano and Vittoria, or feigning madness to divert 'idle questions' (III.2.307), or testing Vittoria's loyalty by convincing her to engage in a suicide pact, he proves himself to be adept at exploiting others for his own purposes, using methods closely allied to the play's more obviously machiavellian characters. His wit, satirical humour, acting ability and lively engagement with the audience, together with his linguistic flexibility as a master of both prose and verse, make him an attractive villain, but villain he undoubtedly is. He commits two murders in the play, of brother and brother-in-law, and shows loyalty to no-one but himself.

In outline, Flamineo's role is a stereotypical one, that of the malcontent. His dissatisfaction and resentment originate in his feelings of undeserved inferiority arising from his perception that his father has squandered his rightful inheritance (see I.2.312–40). His desire for advancement motivates all his actions, notably his vigorous promotion of his sister's relationship with Bracciano, to improve the family's social status. As Bracciano's secretary he remains loyal only when it suits him, and there seems considerable likelihood that he has engaged in financial malpractice, even though this is only hinted at in Bracciano's mad ravings (see V.3.84–87).

Despite his stock role, however, Webster creates in Flamineo a convincing sense of emotional development and an increasing moral awareness, particularly in Act V. As Bracciano lies dying, Flamineo engages in a cynical character assassination of his master to the disguised Francisco, but he is soon filled with a more ominous sense of foreboding about his own mortality (V.3.128–30). He is subsequently overcome with an urge to speak to the dead Bracciano even if he is in hell, and begins to recognise the beginnings of his own moral disintegration: 'I am falling to pieces already' (V.4.25). Unexpectedly, the sight of his brother's corpse being tended by their distracted mother moves him to an uncharacteristic recognition of 'Compassion' and 'conscience' (V.4.116, 122) in himself, and his emotional disintegration is exacerbated by his disturbing encounter with Bracciano's ghost. Though still possessed with a desire for monetary reward, such as 'Vittoria's bounty' (V.4.151), and activated by violent urges — promising to 'drown [his] weapon in her blood' if she doesn't come up trumps (V.4.152) — Flamineo proceeds towards his death with a combination of courage and self-knowledge. His fake death speeches (V.6.100–05 and 138–45) form an interesting contrast with his real ones (V.6.234–76). The former are brittle, conventional and finally melodramatic; the latter are courageous, witty, forgiving, philosophical, satirical and morally aware. Like Vittoria, Flamineo arouses a hugely ambivalent response in the audience.

Bracciano

The play's original title page asserts Bracciano's status as tragic hero. Like all the key players in the drama, he is a deeply ambivalent figure. Referred to as a 'Noble youth' by Francisco (V.2.80), historically he was in his forties during his relationship with Vittoria, and on stage he has been played in various ways, as young and attractive or as an old lecher. There should be a genuine sexual electricity between Vittoria and Bracciano, in order to motivate the murders they instigate to pursue their relationship. Bracciano is presented to the audience in many guises, from the romantic lover, eager and at first a little nervous in anticipating a meeting with his mistress, to the resentful husband, bitter and sarcastic; from the political manipulator, feigning alliances with his enemies, to the generous host, welcoming his guests to the celebration of his second marriage. Key moments in our response to his character are the trial scene, where he seems more concerned with his own dignity than with the plight of his lover, walking out on her in a display of childish petulance; his confrontation with Vittoria in the house of convertites, consumed by jealousy in the face of the apparent love letter from Francisco; and his death scenes, which see him ravaged by madness as the poison consumes his mind and body. There is horror in his death, but little pity, and, unlike conventional tragic heroes, he fails to acquire much in the way of self-knowledge, merely admitting, in the extremity of his anguish, that he is 'too blame' in attacking Flamineo's stewardship, since he himself is just as deserving of censure (V.3.83–90).

In a way, our view of Bracciano is determined partly by Vittoria's love for him, demonstrated in her evident distress during his final agonies where, for once, she seems lost for words. Equally, we can appreciate the more cynical attitude of Flamineo, regaling Mulinassar with an account of Bracciano's ingratitude and disdain for those who serve him (see V.3.56–68). Ultimately, Bracciano is reduced to a mere ghost, a wraith, whose dramatic function is not even the traditional one of demanding revenge for his murder, but merely of indicating to Flamineo the proximity of his own death. The play's moral and emotional complexity does not reside in Bracciano, so that his claim for tragic stature is dubious. Nevertheless, he needs to be played by an actor of presence and charisma.

Francisco de Medici

Francisco is introduced at the start of Act II, immediately after Flamineo's reflections on the 'winding and indirect' ways of 'policy' (I.2.354–55), and in him we see one of the ablest and most devious practitioners of policy in the play. His motives seem to combine family honour, revenge and personal power, and despite his apparent alliance with Monticelso it is clear that he is working principally for his own ends. When it suits him, he can display emotional outrage, as in his first confrontation with Bracciano in Act II scene 1, but he is equally capable of the cool control that he displays during Vittoria's trial in Act III scene 2. News of Isabella's death seems to arouse genuine feelings of grief as he contemplates her young son — 'O, all of my poor sister that remains! / Take him away, for God's sake' (III.2.340–41), but in his brilliant dialogue with Monticelso in Act IV scene 1 he is revealed as the arch-manipulator. He claims that it is 'Far […] from [his] thoughts / To seek revenge' (3–4), and that he is anxious to avoid provoking 'the horrid lust of war' (9), praying that in his 'innocence' he should be free 'from treacherous acts' (22). In a brief soliloquy, however, he reveals that all this is a mere front to conceal his purposes from his former collaborator, and that he is consumed by a slow-burning determination to be revenged (see lines 37–42). As a spur to this revenge, which is partly to be accomplished through the list of murderers in Monticelso's black book, he conjures up Isabella's image in the form of her ghost, but then he angrily dismisses it as a mere irrelevance to his plotting (112–15). Demanding a lighter subplot to his revengeful tragedy (119–20), he aims to provoke Bracciano's jealousy through writing a love letter to Vittoria, and the scene ends with a striking contrast between Francisco's advocacy of cunning rather than strength (131), and his grotesquely violent fantasy of playing football with Bracciano's head (137–38).

Cleverly, Webster creates Francisco's devious nature partly through denying the audience complete access to his motivation and intentions. To our surprise, he is apparently delighted when Vittoria and Bracciano flee the city together, claiming that that, in fact, was the aim of his love letter (IV.3.52–54). His consummate manipulation of Lodovico, convincing him through a trick that, despite Monticelso's threats of damnation, the new Pope actually approves of his involvement in Francisco's revenge plot, is a masterpiece of policy. However, Webster gives us no hint of the most daring element of Francisco's plan, so that when we first see the noble Moor, Mulinassar, welcomed to Bracciano's court in Padua, we should at first not recognise him as Francisco in disguise. As a blunt-speaking, experienced soldier who preaches social equality (see V.1.105–11), Mulinassar is a brilliantly convincing piece of character creation, but there is no particular indication of what Francisco gets out of his direct involvement in the enactment of his revenge plot through his performance skills. His romantic intrigue with Zanche does not really further the plot, except to confirm the details of Isabella's and Camillo's deaths; he takes no part in the actual murder of Bracciano; and he is persuaded to leave Padua before the climactic killings of Vittoria and Flamineo. Webster deliberately engineers Francisco's persistent ambiguity of character and motive, one of the most striking examples being his apparently simultaneous pity and exultation in Bracciano's impending death (V.2.81–84). Strikingly, Francisco escapes moral and legal retribution for his involvement in multiple murders, but the play's moral stance on him is clear in Giovanni's outraged response at the end — 'He turned murderer?' — and his pledge that 'All that have hands in this shall taste our justice' (V.6.290–92), even, perhaps, the uncle who has authorised such violence on his nephew's behalf.

Cardinal Monticelso

Monticelso's character is as ambiguous and contradictory as any in the play. At first, he seems totally in control, adopting a calm, reasonable tone in his moral rebuke of Bracciano for his adulterous behaviour (II.1.26–42), in contrast to Francisco's passionate anger. In his urging of Bracciano to moderate his behaviour for his son's sake (II.1.95–107), we might consider him to be setting a moral example appropriate to his religious status, but it soon becomes clear that he is a devious politician motivated by 'revenge' (II.1.393). His motivation, animated by spite, is laid bare in his justification of the foreign ambassadors' presence at Vittoria's trial, to make her 'black lust […] infamous / To all [the] neighbouring kingdoms' (III.1.7–8). In his management of the trial, unfairly combining the roles of prosecutor and judge as Vittoria points out (III.2.225–26), he loses his calm detachment, building up from a bitter denunciation of Vittoria's status as a typical whore (III.2.78–101) to an almost prurient relish of the details of her assignation with Bracciano at the River Tiber, with their 'wanton bathing and the heat / Of a lascivious banquet' (III.2.196–97). As he allows Vittoria to get the better of him, he descends to sarcasm and a spluttering outrage in the face of her curses and defiance: 'Fie, she's mad […] She's turned Fury' (III.2.275–78). Essentially, though, Monticelso is yet another practitioner of 'policy', urging Francisco to pursue his revenge not by open warfare, but to 'Bear [his] wrongs concealed […] till the time be ripe / For th'bloody audit', in a speech (IV.1.12–21) that stands as an object lesson in how 'policy' operates. Monticelso's hypocrisy is demonstrated in his 'black book' (IV.1.33), an instrument for bribery, blackmail and political control; Francisco is clearly right not to trust him (IV.1.38).

However, Webster leaves an enormous question-mark over Monticelso once he has been elected Pope. His first act is to excommunicate Vittoria and Bracciano — a judgement which clearly has no appreciable effect on the subsequent lifestyle of these 'cursèd persons' (IV.3.67), and which might be interpreted as an early demonstration of his authority or the fulfilment of his private revenge. Subsequently, he wheedles out of Lodovico his involvement in Francisco's murderous plots and threatens him with damnation if he persists, concluding a powerful speech (IV.3.116–27) by urging penitence. These are the words we would expect from a truly religious churchman, but we have no way of knowing whether they represent a genuine change in Monticelso's moral character, to match his visual transformation from the scarlet robes of a cardinal to the white vestments of the Pope, or whether they merely mark him as a still-cunning 'white devil'. We never see him or hear of him again in the play.

Lodovico

Lodovico is a murderer, a lecher and a thug, with virtually no redeeming features, who relishes his acts of violence, almost as a badge of selfhood, from beginning to end of the play. Banished from Rome at the start of the play for 'certain murders' that were 'Bloody and full of horror' (I.1.31–32), even his friends are critical of his dissipated lifestyle, which has ruined himself and others. He is unrepentant, however, vows violent revenge on his enemies (I.1.52–53), and is next heard of as a pirate who hopes to gain Isabella's influence in repealing his banishment (II.1.380–85). He is present when Isabella is poisoned and accompanies Giovanni to Rome, bringing news of her death; strikes up a brief malcontents' pact with Flamineo until he learns that he has been pardoned by the dying Pope; then openly insults Vittoria, for which Flamineo strikes him, instituting a grudge that Lodovico harbours to the very end of the play (see V.6.190). Lodovico seems an unlikely choice to officiate at the papal election, but he is by now in the pay of Francisco, and fully involved in the duke's revenge plots. Another motive of his own is revealed when he confesses to the new Pope that he lusted after Isabella, but in a surprising turn of his character he is apparently persuaded by Monticelso's threats of damnation to 'give [...] o'er' his revenge (IV.3.128). Only Francisco's devious trick of making him believe Monticelso actually approves of his role in the revenge plot restores him to his violent track.

Subsequently, Lodovico accompanies the disguised Francisco to Padua in the guise of a Hungarian Capuchin, and typically imagines various satisfying methods of killing Bracciano, demanding an 'ingenious' plot for which they will be remembered (V.1.75–77). It is Lodovico who poisons Bracciano's helmet and, with Gasparo, administers his final strangulation with gloating relish. It is not clear why he urges Francisco to leave Padua before the remaining murders, except that presumably he does not want to share the glory of revenge with his master. The killing of Flamineo, Vittoria and Zanche is a cowardly act; Flamineo is bound to a pillar and the women have no means of defence. As Vittoria observes with bitter sarcasm, ''Twas a manly blow' (V.6.232), but Lodovico persists in regarding it as a 'most noble deed' (V.6.280). Condemned to torture and imprisonment he remains proudly defiant to the end: 'I do glory yet / That I can call this act mine own' (V.6.294), presenting the scene of carnage, in strikingly effective language, as his crowning masterpiece. He and Giovanni form an intriguingly ambiguous tableau as the play ends, and a production can easily shift the audience's perception of whose moral values ultimately control the world of the play.

Isabella

Isabella's role in the play, though essentially confined to one scene, is interesting and ambiguous. She at first appears as the passive wife, suffering her wrongs with patience and allowing her brother and the Cardinal to negotiate with her adulterous husband. She later greets the erring Bracciano amiably, but his false accusations against her arouse a keen sense of the wrongs she has suffered, and it is difficult to know how to take her protestations that she is neither angry nor jealous. She is shocked when he curses their son and she responds to his vow to divorce her from his bed with passionate feeling and entirely understandable self-pity. Why she decides publicly to take the blame on herself for this separation, though, is unclear. She says it is to 'work peace' between her husband and her brother (II.1.217), but her performance, in which she indulges in a powerfully vindictive attack on her husband's lover, enables her to release her genuine feelings. Webster effectively conveys her impotence in a man's world — 'O that I were a man' (243) — but by adopting her husband's very words and turning them back on him, she is able to acquire something of a man's 'power / To execute [her] apprehended wishes' (243–44). An audience is likely to take an ambivalent view of her in this sequence, but her final lines are genuinely affecting as she faces the prospect of a broken heart provoked by 'the killing griefs which dare not speak' (278). Isabella's death, shown in dumbshow, confirms her as a loving wife, praying before her husband's picture before kissing it three times; and her final appearance, in ghostly form, evokes stillness and silence. In death she is again deprived of the voice she so briefly found to express her anger and anguish.

Camillo

As a stereotype of the cuckolded husband, Camillo brings some light relief to the play's early scenes. He is comically manipulated by his brother-in-law, Flamineo, whose contempt for him is plain to see. A skilful actor can elicit some sympathy for Camillo in his exclusion from his wife's bed and his gullible submission to Flamineo's advice to win his way back there by locking himself away from her. Even his uncle, Monticelso, treats him with disdain, publicly informing him that he is rumoured to be a cuckold and, with Francisco, exploiting him for their own purposes by offering him the entirely inappropriate post of 'commissioner / For the relieving our Italian coast / From pirates' (II.1.360–62). Camillo is at least astute enough to know that this does not seem a particularly good idea, making the best of it with a resolution to get drunk. His death, enacted in dumbshow, can be comic, pathetic or shocking, depending on how it is staged; what it cannot be is tragic.

Cornelia

Webster seems to present Cornelia as a rare focus of moral virtue in the play, but it is a difficult role and can easily turn into a comic stereotype of a ranting old woman — a quality that may well have been exacerbated in the original performances if she were played not by a boy actor but by a mature man. She condemns Vittoria and Bracciano's relationship and curses her daughter, and her language persistently emphasises her status as a mother enduring 'the curse of children' (I.2.281). She will not accept Flamineo's resentment of the family's reduced circumstances as sufficient motive for vice, uttering a forceful moral rebuke in the form of a rhetorical question: 'What? Because we are poor, / Shall we be vicious?'

(I.2.315–16). More generally, she offers an idealised moral statement about princely behaviour (I.2.288–90), employing, as is characteristic of her, an emphatic rhyming couplet. When she returns in Act V, Cornelia maintains her condemnatory role in the face of her children's lustful relationships, this time offering insults and blows to Zanche for her involvement with Flamineo. Her only virtuous child, Marcello, is then taken from her by his brother, toppling her first into emotional denial and subsequently into madness. Again, the task of an actor playing Cornelia is a difficult one if the role is to avoid caricature and achieve pathos. Cornelia's madness is stylised rather than realistic, in a manner that would be instantly recognisable to Webster's audience: the snatches of song, the combination of reason and nonsense, and the handing out of real or imaginary herbs and flowers are strikingly reminiscent of Ophelia's mad scene in *Hamlet*. A clue to the scene's intended impact lies in Flamineo's revelation of the tableau of Cornelia and her ladies tending to Marcello's corpse, in an image similar to a *pietà* (a representation of the body of the crucified Christ being tended by the Virgin Mary). This imparts an air of moral and spiritual virtue to Cornelia and Marcello and suggests that the effect of Cornelia's madness should be quiet and touching rather than shrill or comic.

Zanche

Like the role of Cornelia, that of Zanche is oddly structured. She makes a brief appearance in Act I, is a silent presence in the trial scene, and has an unexpectedly substantial role in Act V. With Flamineo, she observes the first assignation of Vittoria and Bracciano, apparently relishing, in her single line in the scene, their physical embrace: 'See now they close' (I.2.214). There is no indication here that she and Flamineo are themselves engaged in a relationship, though it would be possible to suggest this in performance. Condemned by the authorities as Vittoria's 'bawd' (III.2.264–65), she does not reappear until the wedding celebrations in Padua, where we find her engaged in various sexual intrigues, with Flamineo and subsequently with her supposed countryman, Mulinassar. She is largely a comic figure here, in her undisguised lust for the fake Moor, but she forfeits the audience's sympathy in her betrayal of Vittoria and Bracciano and her intention of robbing her mistress. However, Webster does not develop this strand of the plot, instead transforming Zanche's character in the final scene, first through the resourcefulness with which she helps Vittoria defeat Flamineo's supposed suicide pact, and then in the courage and dignity with which she meets her death. Zanche takes her place in the play as a representative of three oppressed sections of society. As a woman, as a servant and as a member of a racial minority, she suffers demeaning linguistic slurs and contemptuous treatment. In redeeming her at the end of the play, Webster seems to be offering a rebuff to such social, racial and gender prejudices.

Giovanni

The young prince, Giovanni, is in many ways typical of children's roles in Jacobean drama. Combining childish language with a precocious, if naïve, military idealism and a sexual knowingness beyond his years, he could come across as merely irritating to a modern audience. Even in his sorrow for his mother, there is something twee and sentimental about his juvenile apprehension of death — 'What do the dead do, uncle?' (III.2.324) — though in the hands of a gifted boy actor this scene could be both touching and moving. However, by the time he has lost his father too, Webster cleverly invests him with greater maturity and authority, which is first seen in his instinctive distrust of Flamineo and his moral rebuke to him, 'Study your prayers, sir, and be penitent' (V.4.21). His courageous and authoritative control of the play's conclusion carries no echoes of his previous immaturity; his final speeches, in both language and moral judgement, are those of a mature political leader, secure in his administering of justice. There is reason to believe that Webster modelled Giovanni on James I's eldest son, Prince Henry, the heir to the throne. Webster's admiration for Prince Henry was shown in the elegy he wrote on his death later in 1612, *A Monumental Column*, and he celebrated the prince's virtues again in the final section of his 1624 Lord Mayor's pageant, *Monuments of Honour*. Modern directors, however, often sceptical of apparent political virtue, have presented Giovanni as either a fragile boy prince, dominated at the play's close by intimidating adult thugs, or as an adolescent delinquent clearly set to develop into a politician as corrupt and violent as those on view elsewhere in the play (as in the 1991 NT production).

See Sample essay 1 (pages 117–19), for further analysis of Giovanni.

Marcello

The oddest feature of Marcello's role is that we are not told he is Vittoria and Flamineo's brother until his third appearance in the play. At first he appears as Francisco's loyal adjutant, entrusted, jointly with Camillo, with the task of controlling the activities of pirates. As his true identity emerges, however, we find him at odds with his brother over Flamineo's role as pander to Vittoria and Bracciano, yet loyal enough to extricate him from his violent altercation with Lodovico. Presumably banished from Rome along with all Vittoria's family, Marcello shows his resentment in confessing to the disguised Francisco that he has 'thrived [...] poorly' as a soldier (V.1.115–16), and in railing against Flamineo's sexual involvement with Zanche, abusing her both physically and verbally. This culminates in a challenge and in Flamineo's dishonourable killing of Marcello, who regards this as his punishment for the sins of his family, who have 'rise[n] / By all dishonest means' (V.2.21–22). Though Marcello does not create an entirely positive impression on us, the play seems to confirm his essential virtue: he is 'good Marcello' at II.1.366; Francisco is happy to bail him at III.2.255; Hortensio marks his death with the exclamation, 'Virtuous Marcello' at V.2.25; and the *pietà*-like tableau of his dead body tended by Cornelia and her ladies presents him as an almost Christ-like figure. As with other characters, Marcello's impact on the audience can be swayed by the bias given by a particular actor.

Antonelli and Gasparo

There are typical inconsistencies and loose ends in Webster's use of these two characters. Though they are presented in the opening scene as loyal supporters of Lodovico, they are not uncritical of him. They offer him solace, as well as practical help in repealing his banishment, but they also remind him of his crimes and criticise his dissipated lifestyle. Of the two, Gasparo at first seems more disapproving and Antonelli more reassuring, and there is nothing to contradict this impression when they later bring news of the Pope's death-bed pardon for Lodovico. However, in Act V, when they reappear as disguised conspirators with Lodovico in the pay of Francisco, Antonelli's role fades out completely while Gasparo becomes a gleefully vindictive murderer, relishing the power for revenge afforded him by his Capuchin robes as he helps to dispatch Bracciano, and later taking a lead in the killing of Vittoria and her companions. He gives instructions to bind Flamineo to a pillar and offers a cynical observation to Vittoria about princely behaviour (V.6.188–89). There is some scope for an actor to make Gasparo less vicious, in his exhortation to Flamineo to prepare himself for death (V.6.196) and his observation on Vittoria's courage (V.6.219), as well as in his previous comment on Giovanni's qualities (V.4.1). However, in performance he will probably come across simply as one of an undifferentiated gang of contract-killers.

Minor characters

The White Devil is richly endowed with minor characters, who help to root the action in a broad social panorama that embraces domestic servants and attendant ladies; guards and military officers; political and religious functionaries; doctors, lawyers and foreign ambassadors. Frequently, these are employed more as animated scenery than as dramatic characters, as, for example, with the competitors in the '*fight at barriers*' at the start of V.3 (perhaps the same actors as the four **captains** who drink and dance before the killing of Camillo in the second dumbshow in II.2); and the three **ladies** who help to invest Cornelia's tending of Marcello's body with the quality of a *pietà*. The varied array of **servants** helps to create a sense of the working households that support the existence of the play's dukes and nobles; the **Chancellor**, **Register** and **Conclavist**, and even the **Cardinal of Arragon**, create a similar impression of how the political world is serviced; and the various **guards** and **armed men** suggest the military might that underpins power and social position.

Some of the minor characters have more significant roles in the play, while others are given brief but surprising contributions to the dialogue. Doctor **Julio** affords an opportunity for Flamineo to exhibit his satirical wit at its most gross, and provides a moral equation of doctor with murderer, potions with poisons. This is revisited in Flamineo's and Bracciano's contempt for the unfortunate **physicians** who are impotent in the face of the duke's poisoning. The **armourer**, equally, is berated for either complicity or incompetence or both, and his removal to be tortured affords another terrifying demonstration of the operation of power. The **lawyer** is another object of Webster's satire, first because of his offensive wit and then on account of his pompous, inflated and incomprehensible legal terminology. Perhaps there are meant to be two distinct characters here, but the point is doubly effective if we see the same incompetent legal practitioner masking his bawdy colloquialisms before the trial with his inflated pretensions in the courtroom. The **conjurer**, in contrast, is given a surprising sense of moral virtue at the end of his scene, in contrast to his sinister role in conjuring up visions of the murders of Isabella and Camillo.

In Act V, Webster offers us snatches of three characters who could well be combined into one: the young lord of scene 1, the page of scene 2 and the courtier of scene 4. The **young lord** announces the readiness of the combatants in the barriers, perhaps in a pompous and affected manner. When Hortensio asks 'What's he?', Flamineo offers a brief character sketch of this 'new upstart', who seems rather like Osric in *Hamlet* (V.1.145–50). Or perhaps, as John Russell Brown asserts in the Revels Student Edition, they are actually talking here about 'Mulinassar', which would leave the 'young lord' as a totally anonymous character; at any rate, he concludes his role by agreeing to deliver Marcello's sword as a challenge to Flamineo.

The **page** also appears out of nowhere, purely to dispute Cornelia's account of Marcello's death (V.2.68). A page would be a young boy; the question is, whose page is he, and how can he contradict Cornelia's story when he wasn't actually present at Marcello's death? Russell Brown's edition offers a note, not terribly persuasive, on both these issues. Then there is the **courtier** who reports Giovanni's instructions to Flamineo that he is not to come near his presence. Again, there could be a pompous, affected, Osric-like quality to his lines, and doubling him with the young lord would make sense. All three of these characters show Webster providing tiny, significant cameos at a very late stage in the play.

The **matron** of the house of convertites is another brief but effective role. She is wary of the 'damage' she might 'incur' by allowing Bracciano to visit the detained Vittoria (IV.2.3), but does so anyway — perhaps having been bribed by Flamineo. She also receives delivery of the letter to Vittoria from Francisco, which she passes over to Flamineo. An actor in the role could get some mileage out of her slackness here. More important are the six foreign **ambassadors**, who help to frame the play's events in the context of international affairs. They take different views of the court proceedings, and it is notable that not only is the English ambassador the most sympathetic to Vittoria, but that he also escapes Flamineo's sarcastic remarks before the trial, while the Frenchman and the Spaniard are cruelly satirised (III.1.65–78). Perhaps Webster is guiding the audience's response here, and again when the English ambassador explains part of the ritual of the papal election to his French colleague (IV.3.24–32). Although they do not appear on stage, we learn that the ambassadors feel able to honour the marriage of Bracciano and Vittoria with their presence (V.1.57–61), and at the end of the play they are around to protect and support the young Giovanni, with the English ambassador again taking a leading role.

Finally, there are three characters who are introduced in Act V and play a significant role in the play's concluding events. **Carlo** and **Pedro** are supporters of Francisco who have evidently been serving as undercover agents in Bracciano's household; as Francisco earlier admitted, 'Most of [Bracciano's] court are of my faction, / And some are of my counsel' (IV.3.76–77). Both are present to assist Lodovico and Gasparo in the final killings, and Carlo takes on himself the execution of Zanche (V.6.227). **Hortensio** represents the opposing faction, and is a loyal servant of Bracciano. On his first appearance he merely provides a channel for Flamineo to pass on information to the audience about Mulinassar and his companions, but he later acts as a virtuous supporter of Cornelia when Marcello is killed, and is ultimately the agent for the discovery of Francisco's final murder plot — though it seems odd that Webster does not bring him on at the end with the armed 'force' he has presumably 'raise[d]' (see V.5.12–15). A director of the play would almost certainly remedy this omission.

In creating and manipulating all these characters, Webster shows a commanding ability to create a teeming, three-dimensional dramatic world.

Language and style

Some linguistic difficulties

Language is not a fixed entity with a stable and immutable system of signification and usage. New words are created, old ones become redundant, while others change their meaning. Four hundred years is a long time in the life of a language, so it is hardly surprising that we find considerable differences between the language of a Jacobean play and that of today. The 'rules' of modern English spelling, punctuation, grammar and syntax were not really established until the eighteenth century, and in Webster's time language was much more flexible. Frequently we find evidence of a language in flux, with archaic and modern usages working side by side.

The impact of such changes on our understanding of the language of Jacobean drama is often exaggerated, however, and our difficulties with it are sometimes self-fulfilling — we expect it to be difficult, so we find it so. When we listen to the plays

spoken by skilful actors, we understand parts that seemed obscure on the page. We may not grasp the meaning of every word, with all its subtleties of nuance and implication, but we follow the story, understand the characters and their relationships, and appreciate the ideas behind the play.

Often, it is the richness of Webster's metaphorical language that creates a barrier to our immediate understanding. We can be overwhelmed by figurative images at one remove from what is being described or the feelings that are being expressed — images which often tumble one over another in a seemingly unstoppable flow. However, Webster's language is poetry, and we should accept it as such. In responding to poetry, we are required to open our own imaginations to the mysterious power of words to make us see things afresh, from an unlikely angle or a startling perspective. 'Understanding' does not have to be limited to working out a literal meaning; it can be intuitive, imaginative or emotional. The language of poetry enriches us.

Verse and prose

Verse is language that is organised rhythmically according to particular patterns of metre and the arrangement of lines. In plays of Webster's time and earlier, verse was the conventional medium of dramatic discourse. Plays were not regarded as naturalistic slices of life, and the heightened language of verse was felt to be appropriate to their non-realistic status as performance texts. However, dramatists increasingly varied the range of their dramatic language to include speeches and scenes in prose, the language of everyday speech and writing. Verse tended to be given to noble and royal characters, expressing romantic or elevated feelings, while prose was generally used by characters of lower social status, for comic or domestic scenes, for letters read out loud, or to indicate mental disturbance.

Verse

By Webster's time, one particular verse metre had come to dominate the language of plays. This was based on a line of ten syllables, arranged so that the beats, or stresses, fell on every second syllable. Thus, each line consisted of five units (or **metrical feet**), each consisting of an unstressed syllable followed by a stressed one, as follows:

~ /   ~ /   ~ /   ~ /   ~ /

Each of these units is called an iambic foot, and since there are five of them in each line, the metre is called **iambic pentameter**. Here are two typical examples from the play:

~ / ~ / ~ / ~ / ~ /
You see, | my lords, | what good | ly fruit | she seems   (III.2.63)

~ / ~ / ~ / ~ / ~ /
Or I | will drown | this wea | pon in | her blood   (V.4.152)

In the earlier drama of the time, such as Shakespeare's first plays, the rhythms of the iambic pentameter tended to be kept very regular, at the risk of becoming monotonous. As dramatic verse developed, it became more flexible, incorporating an increasing number of irregularities. Two of the most common variations on the basic iambic pentameter are as follows:

(1) An eleventh, unstressed syllable added to a line, giving what is called a feminine ending:

```
 ~  /   ~  /  ~  /  ~  /  ~  /  ~
To be | the ag | ent for | so high | a spi | rit                    (I.2.15)
```

```
 ~   /    ~   /   ~  /   ~ /   ~   /    ~
You came | from thence | a most | notor | ious strum | pet      (III.2.244)
```

(2) Reversing the stresses on the first foot of a line, so that it begins with greater emphasis:

```
 /   ~   ~   /   ~  /  ~ /   ~    /
Zanche | the Moor, | and she | is won | drous proud               (I.2.14)
```

```
 / ~   ~  /   ~ /  ~ /   ~   /
Such a | corrupt | ed tri | al have | you made              (III.2.260)
```

Sometimes both variations occur in the same line:

```
 / ~   ~  /   ~  /   ~   /   ~   /  ~
Let the | caroche | go on, | and 'tis | his pleas | ure               (I.2.8)
```

```
 / ~   ~  /   ~   /   ~   /  ~ /  ~
Terri | fy babes, | my lord | with paint | ed dev | ils           (III.2.147)
```

In passages of dialogue, one verse line can be shared by two speakers. Most editions make this clear by the way the text is set out:

LODOVICO
    I fear I shall be ta'en.
GIOVANNI   You bloody villains,
    By what authority have you committed
    This massacre?
LODOVICO   By thine.
GIOVANNI   Mine?

| LODOVICO | Yes, thy uncle, |
| | Which is a part of thee, enjoined us to't. |

(V.6.283–86)

Again, in early plays, each verse line tended to be a unit of meaning. Later dramatists much more frequently ran the sense of one line into the next, a technique called enjambement; they also created more heavy breaks in the middle of a line, known as caesuras. Both of these have the effect of obscuring rather than emphasising the underlying rhythm of the lines. Look, for example, at Flamineo's speech at V.4.125–52, where the frequent use of truncated lines, enjambement, caesura and metrical irregularity all help to destroy the rhythms of the verse and suggest Flamineo's disturbed state of mind.

Cornelia's dirge over the body of Marcello (V.4.96–105, 108–09) is written in a different and more complex verse form, and is separated from her surrounding speech by italic print in the Revels edition and the New Mermaids 1st edition, but by inverted commas in the New Mermaids 2nd edition. Lines 96–99 rhyme ABBA, with the A-lines in iambic pentameter and the B-lines in trochaic tetrameter. The remaining lines are in rhyming couplets, and are in iambic pentameter, except for lines 100–01 and 108–09, which combine iambic and trochaic tetrameter.

In trochaic metre, each foot is stressed on the first syllable; four feet in a line is tetrameter. Here is a typical line (note: in trochaic metre, the final unstressed syllable of a line is often omitted):

$$/ \sim \; / \sim \; / \sim \; /$$
Call un | to his | funeral | dole

This metre was often used to impart an ominous quality, for example in the speeches of the witches in *Macbeth*. Here, its intermingling with iambic metre creates a combination of chanting, song and poetry, and gives a touching, haunting quality to Cornelia's lament.

If you are writing about the verse of the play or analysing a speech in verse, you need to beware: do not just describe the features of the verse, but analyse and comment on the effects it creates in the lines you are looking at. For example:

- How do regular, fluid verse rhythms create different effects from irregular, broken ones?
- How might an actor respond to the particular features of the verse in developing his or her character?
- What is different about the way the verse is used by different characters, or by the same characters at different times in the play?
- How does the verse work with other language techniques to create the particular effect of a speech?

Prose

Most Jacobean plays contain sections in prose as well as verse, and *The White Devil* is no exception. As already indicated, prose tended to be given to characters of lower social status, and was used in comic or domestic scenes, for the reading aloud of letters, or to indicate mental disturbance. These categories of prose use do not always apply, however, and it is important to establish the particular effects of prose speeches and scenes in the structure of the play as a whole, especially when prose and verse are mingled as freely as they are in this play.

It is a mistake to think that prose is somehow more naturalistic or realistic than verse. Prose can encompass the language of novels, textbooks, newspapers, magazines, letters, diaries and legal documents, and it can be as structured and artificial as verse. It is the everyday language, in speech and writing, of people of varying degrees of education and literacy, and is consequently infinitely varied in its rhythms, grammatical structures and vocabulary.

A number of observations might be made about the use of prose in *The White Devil*:

- Most of the prose of the play is spoken by Flamineo. It distinguishes him in his role as malcontent, and in his feigned madness. It also reflects his consciousness of himself as economically subordinate to others.
- Often, characters who engage in dialogue with Flamineo fall into prose too, even if they are usually verse-speaking characters. This happens particularly with Camillo in I.2.
- Flamineo's speech is not entirely in prose, and he frequently rises to flights of effective and impressive verse, particularly later in the play.
- As befits his status, Francisco de Medici is a verse-speaking character. However, in the early scenes of his disguise as Mulinassar, at the start of Act V, he generally uses prose. This marks him out as 'different' from his usual self, working along with his darkened complexion and Moorish garments. His use of prose, though, contrasts with Flamineo's: it is more formal, more measured, less extravagant in its use of imagery.
- One of the few prose scenes without Flamineo or Francisco is to be found at V.2.28–53, marking Cornelia's grief when Marcello is killed. However, as her passionate anger with Flamineo rises, she reverts to verse at line 54.
- Though Webster could undoubtedly have converted it into verse if he had wished, the Latin of the play is in prose, in the trial scene at III.2.10–11; the papal election at IV.3.43–46 and 59–60; and in Bracciano's death scene at V.3.136–47.

Imagery

An *image* is the mental picture conjured up by a particular word or phrase. When writers use related patterns or clusters of images, they are using *imagery* as a literary technique. Such imagery may serve a number of purposes: it may be a feature of characterisation, infusing characters with particular associations; it may contribute to the creation of mood and atmosphere; or it may support the thematic significance of the text. Webster's use of imagery in *The White Devil* is subtle and pervasive. Among the more notable image clusters, the following are of particular interest and significance:

- nature and the natural environment
- natural phenomena and the weather
- the heavens and heavenly bodies
- animals/birds etc.
- poison and medicine
- make-up and cosmetics
- illness/disease/disablement
- bodily functions
- blood
- death and mortality
- false appearances
- theatre and acting

- murder and revenge
- jewels, precious metals and money
- religion
- policy, politics and politicians
- hell and heaven, angels, devils and furies
- love and lust, sex and sexuality, whores
- colours
- night and darkness
- the law and legal terminology
- confinement and imprisonment
- courtly service and reward
- military activity

When we watch and listen to a performance of the play, we are probably not consciously aware of such verbal patterning, but it will nevertheless help to condition our response. Furthermore, aspects of the imagery are likely to have been taken into account in the design and staging of the production, so that set and costumes, lighting, music and sound effects may well enhance the play's linguistic features. Closer reading and study of the text reveals some of these verbal features in more detail, enabling us to assess their impact at a more consciously analytical level. In writing about imagery, it is therefore important not merely to note image patterns, but to consider the effects they create on our response to the play.

Many of the images listed above are abstract qualities, drawing attention directly to the play's themes, and to the moral and intellectual debate in which the characters are engaged. This applies to ideas such as revenge, mortality, policy and false appearances. Other images are more visceral in their impact, creating an awareness of human beings as mere animals with certain bodily needs and functions, subject to illness and disablement, sexual drives, death and decay. Then there are images that put the play's moral and religious debate into a metaphorical or emblematic context. The key idea of moral hypocrisy, for example, is developed through images drawn from the semantic field of theatre and performance, as well as from the religious symbolism of heaven and hell, angels and devils. Patterns of imagery often collide and coexist, offering the reader or listener a complex web of interlinked associations. In a striking example,

Monticelso's characterisation of a whore ranges through an antithetically constructed image sequence incorporating perfumes and poisons, death and decay, weather and climate, bodily needs, hell and sin, counterfeit money and legal trickery, constantly returning to the central issue of false appearances (see III.2.78–101). A passage such as this demonstrates in microcosm something of Webster's method throughout the whole play.

Structure

The structure of *The White Devil* has frequently been criticised. Even an admirer of the play such as John Russell Brown claims that 'the plot or structure of *The White Devil* is loose and rambling, a gothic aggregation rather than a steady exposition and development towards a single consummation'. This seems unfair. What Webster offers, like so many playwrights of the period, is a play that almost deliberately seems to eschew the classical clarity of the unities — Aristotle's 'rules' demanding a single plot unfolding in a single location within a single day. Instead, Webster creates a variety of structural features superimposed on one another.

Two parts

We do not know whether open-air theatres such as the Globe or the Red Bull had intervals in their performances. What is clear is that many plays of the period have an obvious place for such an interval, roughly two-thirds of the way through and often coinciding with the end of Act III. In *The White Devil*, such a break would be more appropriate after Act IV, since Act V is exceptionally long. Such a two-part structure reflects the play's two settings. Part I (Acts I–IV) takes place in Rome, focuses on the development of Vittoria and Bracciano's relationship and culminates in their flight from the house of convertites. Part II (Act V) finds them married and on Bracciano's home turf in Padua, but presents their idyll infiltrated by the disguised Francisco and his confederates and shows the working out of their revenge plot. Incidentally, this structure, with a short break between the two parts, would allow plenty of time for the practicalities of costume and make-up changes required to transform Francisco into Mulinassar.

Four movements

Although he ignores the unities, Webster does construct the plot according to an alternative neoclassical model, in which there are four movements. In the first movement, the *protasis* or exposition, the characters are introduced and the basic situation set up. Act I provides a kind of double exposition in this case, establishing the identity and motivation of Lodovico, and introducing the relationship between Bracciano and Vittoria. In the second movement, or *epitasis*, complications begin to arise, as they do in Webster's Act II, with the unsuccessful intervention of

Monticelso and Francisco in the marriage of Bracciano and Isabella. The third movement, or *catastasis,* develops increasing complexities and builds to a climax; again, Webster doubles the impact with the dual climax of Vittoria's trial and the papal election, two set-piece, ceremonial scenes. Finally comes the *catastrophe,* in which the complications of the plot are resolved — in this case through multiple killings — and order is restored.

Five acts

Although we are used to reading playtexts of Shakespeare and Webster's time divided into five acts, for many plays of the period this is an artificial convention bearing little relationship to the plots of the plays, and performances in the outdoor theatres were more-or-less continuous. However, by 1612 the leading adult companies were also playing in indoor theatres, which made different demands on dramatic structure. Here, the need to trim excess wax at regular intervals from the candles that lit the theatre led to a deliberate five-act structuring of the plays written for such venues. After each act there was a break, during which music would be played while the candles were attended to. Although *The White Devil* was first performed at an open-air theatre, Webster may well have hoped and planned for a presentation at one of the more prestigious indoor houses such as the Blackfriars — something he later achieved with *The Duchess of Malfi.* Thus, he caters for such a possibility with a clear-cut five-act structure. The Act I exposition climaxes in Vittoria's suggestive dream, Cornelia's outrage and Flamineo's statement of his motivation. Act II builds up to the visual climax of the murders, staged in dumbshow, of Isabella and Camillo. Act III centres on Vittoria's trial. Act IV focuses on the argument and reconciliation between Vittoria and Bracciano, and builds to the climax of the papal election and the establishing of Lodovico as the agent of revenge. And Act V unravels the whole plot in a sequence of violent killings before the restoration of order as Giovanni takes command.

It is notable that in all three of these structural analyses of the play, Act V stands by itself, and Webster has done a great deal to achieve this. Its separateness as a dramatic unit is marked by the change of setting from Rome to Padua; the disappearance of Monticelso from the action; the reimagining of Francisco in the guise of Mulinassar, with his disguised companions; the introduction of significant minor characters such as Carlo, Pedro and Hortensio; the major developments in the roles of Cornelia and Zanche; and the fact that all the deaths in the play, apart from those in the dumbshows, are clustered here: Marcello, Bracciano, Zanche, Vittoria, Flamineo. However one looks at the play, it is clear that the dramatist exerts a conscious control over the structuring of the plot, which is very far from the 'loose and rambling' edifice suggested by John Russell Brown.

Themes

The themes of a literary text may or may not have been developed consciously by the author. Usually, we have no means of knowing an author's intentions; what is important is the impact of the text on a reader or, in the case of a play, an audience. Even if an author has written explicitly about the thematic content of a work, that does not preclude other themes from coming to the attention of particular readers.

Responding to the themes of a complex drama such as *The White Devil* is not as simple as asking what the 'moral' of the play is. The themes range across personal relationships, social structures, religious and political morality and philosophical reflections on the meaning of life; they are developed through a web of overlapping and interconnecting ideas and are made evident through plot and narrative, characterisation, language and imagery.

Violence and revenge

In some of the earlier revenge tragedies of the Elizabethan and Jacobean period, there is a central revenger whose motivation is established early in the play: Hieronimo in *The Spanish Tragedy*, the title character in *Hamlet* and Vindice in *The Revenger's Tragedy* are striking examples. Those plays chart the progress of the protagonists' revenge and show how it leads them into morally murky waters. The revenge theme in *The White Devil* is not so clear-cut, partly because there are multiple motives and multiple revengers. Lodovico swears revenge on all those of his enemies whom he perceives as being responsible for his banishment ('I'll make Italian cut-works in their guts / If ever I return', I.1.52–53), but seems equally fired by the pleasure of revenging a minor blow inflicted on him by Flamineo ('Sirrah, you once did strike me; I'll strike you / Into the centre', V.6.190–91). Monticelso has no scruples about seeking revenge on Bracciano for dishonouring his nephew ('For my revenge I'd stake a brother's life', II.1.393) and subsequently for that nephew's murder, and is surprised when Francisco claims it to be 'Far [...] from [his] thoughts / To seek revenge' for his sister's death (IV.1.3–4), urging him to plan for the 'bloody audit' (IV.1.19). However, after his election as Pope, we find him dissuading Lodovico from participating in Francisco's revenge on the grounds that ''tis damnable'; 'Dost thou imagine', he asks, '[that] thou canst slide on blood / And not be tainted with a shameful fall?' (IV.3.118–19). This seems a strange moral reversal for Monticelso's character, contributing to the play's increasingly complex discussion of revenge.

It is, in the event, Francisco's revenge that is pursued with the most single-minded determination, though he avoids all personal involvement in the killings, leaving them to his gang of contract-killers. He bemoans the underhand methods employed in Bracciano's murder: 'methinks that this revenge is poor, / Because it

steals upon him like a thief' (V.1.79–80). To Francisco, revenge should be a 'glorious act' that brings 'fame' (V.5.9–10). His desire for 'part of the glory' (IV.3.79) explains his need to be present during the final stages of his revenge, against Lodovico's advice, though ultimately he is persuaded by Lodovico to leave Padua before the killings are over. Revenge, for Francisco, has nothing to do with achieving justice; 'What harms it justice?' he demands, emphasising again that 'fame / Shall crown the enterprise' (V.3.269–71).

In contrast to earlier revenge tragedies, *The White Devil* offers no explicit moral statements on the issue of revenge — at least, none that we can trust. However, the play's conclusion perhaps makes Webster's position clear. Giovanni is unmoved by the fact that the climactic 'massacre' (V.6.285) has been committed on his own behalf and instigated by his uncle. To the young prince, the demands of 'justice' are clear, requiring 'prison' and 'torture' for all who were involved in such a bloody revenge (291–92). The play ends with Giovanni's salutary warning to those who live by violence, in what may be seen as an apt moral conclusion to the revenge theme:

> Let guilty men remember their black deeds
> Do lean on crutches, made of slender reeds. (V.6.300–01)

Social class

Flamineo is motivated partly by resentment at his family's social position, and the issue of social class is a recurrent motif in the play. Monticelso acknowledges that Vittoria is 'honourably descended / From the Vitelli' (III.2.235–36), but makes it clear that her family's inherited wealth has been dissipated, so that she brought 'not one julio' in dowry from her father when she married Camillo (III.2.241). Her diminished social status, he says, was matched by her moral status, since she 'came from [Venice] a most notorious strumpet' (III.2.244). An unsympathetic interpretation of her relationship with Bracciano might put it down to social climbing on her part; as Monticelso sarcastically points out, 'she did counterfeit a prince's court' (III.2.75).

As Flamineo earlier made clear, the blame for the family's social downfall can be laid at the door of their father, whose dissipated lifestyle frittered away the family fortune (see I.2.318–20). Flamineo is clearly eaten up with resentment at his demeaning career as a poor student and now a poor secretary, leading to his obsessive drive to seek 'preferment' (I.2.330) in order to raise his 'beard out of the level / Of [his] lord's stirrup' (I.2.314–15). To him, this justifies any course of action, however immoral, and it is left to his mother to take a more principled view of their social position: 'What? Because we are poor, / Shall we be vicious?' (I.2.315–16). Marcello, at his death, clearly blames it on his siblings' irresponsible and immoral social aspirations: 'This it is to rise / By all dishonest means' (V.2.21–22).

Through the example of Flamineo and his family, social inequality is seen as an evil inasmuch as it can lead to dissatisfaction and criminality. Mulinassar, the Moor, takes a more abstract view, explicitly preaching the equal value of all human beings, regardless of their social class. He uses the analogy of building: it is a mere matter of chance whether a brick is placed 'on the top of a turret' or 'in the bottom of a well'; thus, he argues, there is no difference between himself and the duke, whatever their position in society (V.1.105–11). Our response to these views is complicated, of course, by the fact that the supposedly blunt soldier, Mulinassar, is in fact Duke Francisco in disguise. Nevertheless, the points he makes have been laid out for our consideration.

Religion

One might naively assume that a churchman, particularly one invested with high office, should be a repository of spirituality and moral virtue. The example of Cardinal Monticelso, later Pope Paul IV, demonstrates instead the prevalence of religious hypocrisy. He is a worldly politician, aiming to outmanoeuvre his enemies and even his allies to achieve and consolidate power and exact revenge. In a wonderful irony, he has a book in which 'lurk / The names of many devils' (IV.1.35–36); as Francisco wryly points out using a theological term, this is a 'strange doctrine' (IV.1.67). A similar irony is at work when Lodovico, and later Carlo, are said to have taken 'the sacrament' (IV.3.72, V.1.64) in vowing to enact Francisco's bloody revenge. Though Monticelso, as Pope, preaches damnation to Lodovico if he persists in his violent course, urging him 'by [his] penitence [to] remove this evil, / In conjuring from [his] breast that cruel devil' (IV.3.126–27), Webster never makes it clear whether his elevation to the papacy has imbued him with a new spirituality; it is significant that Lodovico is easily persuaded to believe the Pope's hellfire preaching was a mere front. Constantly, the play and its characters emphasise how figures of religious authority repeatedly fall short of moral virtue, from Vittoria's assertion that 'charity' is 'seldom found in scarlet' (III.2.70–71) to Flamineo's more general observation that 'there's nothing so holy but money will corrupt and putrify it' (III.3.27) followed by his even more forceful observations that religion is 'commeddled with policy' and that 'The first bloodshed in the world happened about religion' (III.3.38–40). The theme is summed up in images such as the broken crucifix (V.2.11–13), suggesting not just the fraternal rift between Flamineo and Marcello, but the fracture of religious principles endemic to the play's Catholic society. It is emphasised, too, in Lodovico and Gasparo's disguise as Capuchin monks, using their robes, '*crucifix and hallowed candle*' (V.3.130SD) as a front for their vicious and vindictive revenge; they are even able to administer the last rites to Bracciano in an impressive Latin ritual.

The question arises as to whether the play gives any sense of a true spirituality and religious virtue that exists above and beyond its debased practitioners. Such hints are infrequent and fragile. There is the moving spectacle of Cornelia and her ladies '*winding* MARCELLO's *corse*' (V.4.65SD), in a tableau deliberately reminiscent of a *pietà*. And there is, perhaps, the character of the young Giovanni, urging Flamineo: 'Study your prayers, sir, and be penitent' (V.4.21) and contextualising his stern punishment of the murderers at the end of the play with the afterthought, 'As I hope heaven' (V.6.293).

Love and lust

Relationships between the sexes are not presented in a particularly positive light in *The White Devil*. Camillo is excluded from his wife's bed, is consumed with jealousy and ultimately has to acknowledge his pathetic status as cuckold. Isabella is the victim of a loveless husband and has her reconciliatory overtures turned back in her face, so that she has to take the blame for their separation on herself. Where any ideal of love might lie in these two marriages is difficult to see, though Isabella continues to perform the ritual of kissing her husband's picture before going to bed, thus meeting her death. It is her love, perhaps, that kills her.

More powerful than love is the lust that drives Vittoria and Bracciano into the sins of adultery and murder. Even the superficially romantic language of their first encounter is couched in terms of sexual innuendo ('you shall wear my jewel lower', I.2.228), and their relationship is stigmatised by society as what Francisco calls 'curst dotage' (II.1.389). Yet there is hypocrisy in society's attitude to the lovers, combining as it does moral condemnation with a prurient fascination evident in Monticelso's apparent relish of their 'wanton bathing and the heat / Of a lascivious banquet' (III.2.196–97). Typically for the time, Vittoria, as a woman, is condemned as a whore while Bracciano, the man, largely escapes with a ticking off — an attitude Vittoria attempts to reverse in her vigorous self-defence:

> Grant I was tempted;
> Temptation to lust proves not the act.
> [...]
> You read his hot love to me, but you want [i.e. lack]
> My frosty answer. (III.2.198–202)

Lust, adultery and murder combine to ensure that the relationship of Vittoria and Bracciano is no easier than the marriages they have betrayed. He abandons her to the judgement of the court, and their meeting in the house of convertites is marked by angry recriminations. However, the progress of the plot, with their eventual marriage implicitly sanctioned by the foreign ambassadors, suggests that genuine love develops between them. Thus, in the face of Bracciano's poisoning, Vittoria is shown to be distraught at the fate of her 'loved lord' (V.3.7) while he bemoans how little he has been able to give to 'this good woman': 'Had I infinite worlds / They were too little for thee' (V.3.17–18). At his death, there is no doubting the depth

of Vittoria's grief: 'O me! This place is hell' (V.3.180) — despite Flamineo's cynically misogynistic commentary, 'There's nothing sooner dry than women's tears' (V.3.187). Interestingly, Vittoria barely refers to Bracciano in the final scene of the play; when she does, she exalts their relationship to the level of religious worship, inviting us to make our own judgement on the nature of love:

> Behold, Bracciano, I that while you lived
> Did make a flaming altar of my heart
> To sacrifice unto you, now am ready
> To sacrifice heart and all.   (V.6.83–86)

Even if we accept that lust is transformed into love in the play's central relationship, no such metamorphosis takes place elsewhere in the play. With cynical economy, Webster points out the fine line between love and lust in Lodovico's admission to the Pope:

> Sir, I did love Bracciano's duchess dearly;
> Or rather I pursued her with hot lust.   (IV.3.111–12)

Sexual love in the play is balanced by the theme of maternal love, explored through the figures of Isabella and Cornelia. Only after her death is Isabella's love for her son made clear, through Giovanni's sense of loss. Through him we learn that, rather than employing a wet nurse as was the custom for most ladies of the nobility, she breast-fed the baby Giovanni herself; as he comments, 'it should seem by that she dearly loved me' (III.2.338). As the mother of three contrasting and troublesome children, Cornelia's maternal instincts are more complex. She also breast-fed at least one of her children, Flamineo (see V.2.11–13), but this was probably more to do with her diminished social status. Marcello is clearly her favourite child, partly because he evidently shares her profession of moral virtue; as for the others, they arouse in her an anguished recognition of 'the curse of children', who 'In life [...] keep us frequently in tears, / And in the cold grave leave us in pale fears' (I.2.281–83). When Marcello is killed, Cornelia's 'tears' and 'fears' are exacerbated by the fact that her other son is responsible. Her grief is movingly portrayed, as are her contradictory feelings towards the surviving, fratricidal son, whom she instinctively attacks with a knife before concluding that she cannot face losing him too. Love in the play, whether sexual or maternal, is seen as the source of both joy and pain.

False appearances

As the play's title makes clear, false appearances are thematically central to its moral concerns. As Iago notes with gleeful self-satisfaction in *Othello*, 'When devils will the blackest sins put on, / They do suggest at first with heavenly shows' (*Othello*, III.1.343). So little in *The White Devil* is as it seems that the moral force of the title pervades the entire play, suggesting a world where false appearances are assumed as a matter of course, from the protestations of virtue espoused by the adulterous Vittoria to the actual disguises adopted by Francisco and his murderous henchmen. So powerful is the theme of false appearances and hypocrisy that many critics, directors and audiences even refuse to take the apparent virtue of Isabella, Cornelia, Marcello and Giovanni at face value — and there is enough textual evidence to justify such a response.

This central theme is supported by plot, characterisation and a web of imagery, only a fraction of which can be examined here. Vittoria herself is often the focus of such images. To Flamineo she is an 'Excellent devil' (I.2.257) for the craft with which she exploits her supposed dream; to Monticelso, she 'seems' like 'goodly fruit' but is actually bitter to the taste like the apples growing on the site of the unholy cities of Sodom and Gomorrah (III.2.63–65); subsequently he blazes her whoredom to the court in a series of metaphors of false appearance, from 'poisoned perfumes' to 'counterfeited coin' (III.2.81, 99) and, later, 'counterfeit jewels' (III.2.141). She defends herself against the charge of being a 'painted devil' (III.2.147), turning Monticelso's accusations back on him by 'discern[ing] poison / Under [his] gilded pills' (III.2.190–91). Unmoved, he maintains his assertions of her disguised evil: 'If the devil / Did ever take good shape, behold his picture' (III.2.216–17). In one of the most vivid images of this verbal patterning, even Bracciano condemns the discrepancy between the real Vittoria and her outward appearance: 'How long have I beheld the devil in crystal?' (IV.2.88)

However, Vittoria is far from being the only purveyor of false appearances in the play. Images drawn from the semantic field of theatrical performance are frequent reminders of the unreliability of outward show, and many characters in the play are consciously acting a role: Isabella in her appropriation of Bracciano's words to present herself as the causer of their marital rift; Francisco in his disguise as Mulinassar with Lodovico and Gasparo in their roles as Capuchin monks; and Flamineo, both in his assumed madness and his fake death. Francisco's romantic love letter to Vittoria conceals his vengeful intentions, and the need to conceal inner reality from too close a scrutiny drives most of the characters to adopt strategies of deceit and concealment. In a world where spying on others seems endemic, demonstrated in the number of scenes where events are viewed by one or more observers, such behaviour is vital to success and even survival.

Policy

Webster constantly makes us think about the ways in which powerful people acquire and maintain their power. Rarely are their methods as straightforward as using outright force and open violence; instead, he shows them operating through 'policy', a combination of strategies based on scheming, deceit and manipulation. As Flamineo states early in the play, the ways of policy are 'winding and indirect'

(I.2.355). Anyone who employs such methods might be described as 'politic', or as a 'politician', and in *The White Devil* these methods are not confined to those characters who have most power. Flamineo himself and his sister Vittoria are as adept at employing policy and its devious strategies as Bracciano, described on his deathbed as 'You that were held the famous politician; / Whose art was poison' (V.3.155–56) — a poison now operating in his own 'politic brains' (V.3.164).

The most powerful practitioners of policy in the play, however, are Francisco and Monticelso. Their covert, underhand tactics are constantly in evidence, providing the audience with a kind of practical manual of policy and its operation. For their initial manipulation of Bracciano, they work cleverly as a team, playing off Francisco's emotional outrage against Monticelso's calm reasonableness in what Flamineo describes as their 'invisible cunning' (II.1.288). Their teamwork only survives, however, as long as their objectives coincide, and in Act IV scene 1 they play a game of cat-and-mouse in which their true aims are concealed from each other. Monticelso recommends that Francisco should pursue his revenge through craft and policy, since 'undermining more prevails / Than doth the cannon' (IV.1.13–14). Francisco pretends to be outraged — 'Free me my innocence, from treacherous acts!' (IV.1.22) — while secretly planning just the kind of politic methods advocated by his former partner, from whom he is determined to conceal them, reflecting that Monticelso '[cannot] reach what I intend to act' (IV.1.40). The word 'policy' and its derivatives are reiterated throughout the play, repeatedly illustrated by practical examples of its operation. In developing this theme, Webster offers a cynical exposé of how society functions.

See also Sample essay 2 (pages 119–21) for a more detailed account of the theme of policy in the play.

Madness

Madness is a favourite theme of Renaissance dramatists, and one that is explored in some of the period's greatest plays, such as *Hamlet* and *King Lear*. The plays of Webster and Middleton create a world in which the apparently sane are as mad as those confined in the asylums portrayed on stage in both *The Duchess of Malfi* and *The Changeling*.

In *The White Devil*, Webster presents the feigned madness of Flamineo, the grief-induced madness of Cornelia and the terrifying madness of Bracciano, his brain eaten away by poison. Each is portrayed according to the dramatic conventions of the period. Flamineo's 'mad humour' (III.2.306) takes the form of a kind of hyper-active extension of his role as malcontent, raving about the injustices of society that he blames for his sister's public humiliation. Often, it is difficult to distinguish between his assumed madness and his normal character; it is simply that, like Hamlet, his mad guise gives him the licence to express his deep social resentment more openly. Webster pays homage to *Hamlet*, too, in basing much of Cornelia's mad scenes on those of Ophelia. Both are grief-crazed, Ophelia for the fact that her father has been killed by her lover, Cornelia for the killing of one of her sons by his own brother. Both characters combine nonsense with snatches of song or verse; both give out real or imaginary herbs and flowers including rosemary, for remembrance; both convey a combination of touching sadness with painful embarrassment; and both exit bidding farewell to the assembled company.

Bracciano's mad scene is altogether more volatile, befitting its violent circumstances, as he veers between nonsense, incisive awareness, bitter social commentary, hallucinations, and lunatic laughter. It is scenes such as this that help to imbue the play with its Gothic atmosphere, but the emphasis on madness goes further, causing us to question 'the sanity […] of the whole state' (*Hamlet*, I.3.21). As Middleton's Vindice says: 'Surely we are all mad people, and they / Whom we think are, are not' (*The Revenger's Tragedy*, III.5.80–81).

The play in performance

Early productions

As Webster himself tells us in his preface to the printed text of *The White Devil*, the play's first performance in 1612 had not been a success, despite apparently having been well acted by the Queen's Men, especially Richard Perkins who probably played Flamineo. Webster blamed its failure on the 'open and black' Red Bull Theatre, its ignorant and undiscerning audiences, and the fact that the play was presented in bleak winter weather.

Despite its initial failure, the play was revived a number of times, both during the reign of Charles I, and later in the century when the theatres were reopened after the Civil War, following the restoration to the monarchy of Charles II. This was the period in which women were allowed to perform on the public stage for the first time. The famous diarist, Samuel Pepys, saw the play on 2 October 1661 and didn't enjoy it — but this seems to have been more on account of his late arrival and poor seat than because of the quality of the play and performance. Oddly, he went back 2 days later to see 'a bit of' the play again, and enjoyed it even less!

Modern revivals

As far as we know, the play was not performed again until the early twentieth century, when there was a revival of interest not only in the plays of Shakespeare's contemporaries, but also in early modern theatre practice. The productions of 1925 and 1935, however, were assessed mainly for their curiosity value, and few critics were convinced of the play's greatness.

The first major production of the century was given at the Duchess Theatre in 1947, directed by Michael Benthall. Vittoria was played by Margaret Rawlings and

Flamineo by Robert Helpmann, and this time the critics were more impressed, with both the play and the staging. It followed on from a revival of *The Duchess of Malfi* in 1945, and both productions benefited, if that is not an inappropriate word, from the immediate post-war revelations of the horrific genocide of the Holocaust. Somehow, in such a context, Webster's horrors no longer seemed so artificial, literary and extravagant.

By the mid-1950s, the increasing fashion for modern-dress presentations of classic plays was applied to *The White Devil* in a New York production that linked it to the seedy atmospherics of the tough detective novel or the Hollywood genre of *film noir*. By now, the play was becoming famous enough, too, to be produced by student companies and amateur groups as well as regional theatres.

There were a number of notable productions in the second half of the twentieth century. Frank Dunlop directed the play for the National Theatre at the Old Vic in 1969, with Geraldine McEwan as Vittoria and Edward Woodward as Flamineo. Extravagantly set and costumed, this created a world of conspicuous display undermined by corruption and decay. For many critics, it evoked Rupert Brooke's description of Webster's world as being 'full of the feverish and ghastly turmoil of a nest of maggots'.

In 1976, Michael Lindsay-Hogg directed a modern-dress production, also at the Old Vic, in a text prepared by the playwright Edward Bond, whose plays explore a world of shockingly cool, clinical violence. Glenda Jackson was Vittoria and Jack Shepherd Flamineo. The set suggested the foyer of a stylish hotel, with characters entering and leaving through swing doors, and Lodovico, for example, clearly ready to catch his plane into banishment at the start. There was a distinctly feminist slant to this production, and an interesting tension between the contemporary world it conjured up and the distinctively Jacobean qualities of Webster's play.

The National Theatre returned to the play, at its Olivier Theatre, in 1991, in a production by the controversial director-designer Philip Prowse, who created an extravagant setting of vast tombs, altars and basilicas, simultaneously grand and ruined. Sinister, hooded monks and wandering ghosts haunted the fringes of the action, and the production's atmospherics included tolling bells, flickering candles and rumbling thunder. Most notably, the status of Vittoria and her family was heightened by casting black actors in the roles, including Josette Simon as Vittoria and Dhobi Oparei as Flamineo. This proved controversial, though for many reviewers it clarified, in particular, Flamineo's resentment at his subsidiary social position. Prowse's grandly operatic and Gothic style, however, was generally not liked.

Probably the best production in recent years was that by Gale Edwards for the Royal Shakespeare Company in 1996. This benefited from its staging in smaller, more intimate theatres: firstly, the Swan, a galleried Jacobean-style playhouse in Stratford-upon-Avon, and later the Barbican Centre's Pit theatre in London, a claustrophobic, underground studio space. The production was fast, clear, colourful, stylish and, according to the reviewers, oozing sweaty sexuality. It was finely acted by a company including Jane Gurnett as Vittoria, Ray Fearon as Bracciano, Philip Voss as Monticelso and Stephen Boxer as Francisco, but it was Richard McCabe's Flamineo that captured the true Websterian combination of wit, corruption, seedy sexuality, linguistic flair, comic energy, burning resentment, and a flippant rapport with the audience.

Up to now (2008), *The White Devil* has not had a major twenty-first-century production.

Critical debate

The play and the critics

The concept of Elizabethan and Jacobean plays as objects of critical scrutiny did not really emerge until the eighteenth century. Earlier critical attitudes were implicit in the theatrical representation of the plays, particularly in adaptations which radically altered them to conform with contemporary notions of taste and decorum.

With the gradual emergence of Shakespeare as unassailable 'national poet', the work of his contemporaries was inevitably relegated to subsidiary status. The plays of Marlowe, Jonson, Middleton and Webster were judged against the 'genius' of Shakespeare and found wanting.

During the Romantic period of the early nineteenth century, there were a number of critics who found much to praise in Webster, among them Charles Lamb, William Hazlitt and Sir Walter Scott. Due admiration was offered to the incidental beauties of Webster's poetic style and the force of his tragic vision, but commentators were worried by what they saw as the violent excesses and dubious morality of the plays, and criticised their perceived structural weaknesses.

In the twentieth century there was renewed interest in Elizabethan and Jacobean drama, with influential and enthusiastic studies of Webster offered by, for example, the poets Rupert Brooke and T. S. Eliot. Often, though, Webster was analysed in the context of revenge tragedy or the tragedy of blood, his plays losing something of their individuality by being linked with those of playwrights such as Middleton, Tourneur and Ford. Twentieth-century critics found particular relevance in these plays when set against the appalling horrors of global warfare. Though Shakespeare remained the touchstone against which they were judged, there was an increasing appreciation, particularly in the 1960s, of their disturbing generic mix, their horror inextricably bound up with gruesome comedy.

Perhaps critical assessments of Jacobean drama tell us more about the critics than about the plays. Critical theory has now become a bewildering web of conflicting orthodoxies in which not only the text but the student may well get left behind. While many examiners at AS and A-level still promote a kind of liberal humanist approach to literature which prioritises an informed personal response engendered and validated by close textual scrutiny, the specifications themselves now emphasise the contextualisation of texts both in the historical, social and political climate that produced them, and in the critical debate of succeeding ages.

Much of value can be gained from a variety of modern critical approaches. For example, **political criticism**, which might include **Marxist** analysis and **new Historicism**, reminds us that literary texts are products of a particular set of socio-political circumstances from which they cannot be divorced, and that they are informed by a range of cultural preoccupations and anxieties that manifest themselves whether they are consciously intended by the writer or not. Social and political issues are crucial to *The White Devil*, from the machiavellian plotting of Francisco and Monticelso, with its statements about power and religion, to the anxieties about social status relating to Flamineo and his family.

Feminist criticism, similarly, challenges assumptions about gender and exposes both the sexual stereotyping embodied in a text and the way in which such stereotypes might be subverted. Whether Webster's plays exhibit feminist sympathies or whether they merely accept and endorse the patriarchal status quo and the misogyny of their time is an issue that can only enhance a consideration of the roles of Vittoria, Isabella, Cornelia and Zanche.

Other critical ideologies focus on language rather than social and historical context, and are closely based on complex issues of linguistic philosophy that can make them difficult for a non-specialist to grasp. **Structuralism** and **post-structuralism** see the relationship between language and meaning (or **signifier** and **signified**) as essentially fluid and shifting, revealing contradiction and ambivalence to such a degree that interpretation becomes no more than an identification of an ever-expanding range of possible meanings. In this context, as Roland Barthes suggests, the role of the author is irrelevant, and any concept of authorial intention or control is a mere chimera. What this does not mean, however, is that a text can mean anything we want it to.

Deconstruction is a broad term, but its adherents are particularly adept at interrogating texts to find their contradictions and ambiguities, their generic discontinuities and their revealing gaps and silences. Deconstructionist critics often arrive at challenging and controversial interpretations which may seem perverse but have the merit of sending us back to the text to question it for ourselves.

Performance criticism looks at how the form of dramatic texts is determined by their basis in theatrical practice, examining them against what is known of the original stage conditions for which they were produced and the way they have been represented subsequently in other theatres and performance media. Such an approach questions the notion of a definitive text and undermines the concept of authorship, since theatre is essentially collaborative and ephemeral.

Presentism is a recent critical movement that embraces the necessity of interpreting texts from the past in the light of our own present-day attitudes and experiences. Whereas previous critical ideologies tried to avoid imposing modern cultural attitudes on such genres as Jacobean drama, presentism welcomes such an approach as both inevitable and invaluable.

In practice, most critical analysis, including your own, will be a synthesis of different critical methods and approaches.

The following quotations represent a range of critical approaches to the play:

> This White Devil of Italy sets off a bad cause so speciously, and pleads with such an innocence-resembling boldness, that we [...] are ready to expect, when she has done her pleadings, that her very judges, her accusers, the grave ambassadors who sit as spectators, and all the court, will rise and make proffer to defend her in spite of the utmost conviction of her guilt.   Charles Lamb, 1808

> This play is so disjointed in its action, — the incidents are so capricious and so involved, — and there is, throughout, such a mixture of the horrible and the absurd — the comic and the tragic — the pathetic and the ludicrous, — that we find it impossible [...] to give any thing like a complete and consistent analysis of it.   'H. M.', 1818

> In the trial scene in particular, [Vittoria's] sudden indignant answers to the questions that are asked her, startle the hearers. Nothing can be imagined finer than the whole conduct and conception of this scene [...]. The sincerity of her sense of guilt triumphs over the hypocrisy of their affected and official contempt for it.   William Hazlitt, 1820

> To us the knowledge of character shown in Vittoria's trial-scene, is not an insight into Vittoria's especial heart and brain, but a general acquaintance with the conduct of all bold bad women when brought to bay.
>   Charles Kingsley, 1856

> When we find a playwright [...] drenching the stage with blood [...] and searching out every possible circumstance of horror — ghosts, maniacs, severed limbs and all the paraphernalia of the charnel-house and the tomb — with no conceivable purpose except just to make our flesh creep, may we not reasonably, or rather must we not inevitably, conclude that he either revelled in 'violent delights' for their own sake, or wantonly pandered to the popular craving for them?   William Archer, 1893

> A play of Webster's is full of the feverish and ghastly turmoil of a nest of maggots. [...] Human beings are writhing grubs in an immense night. And the night is without stars or moon. But it has sometimes a certain quietude in its darkness; but not very much.   Rupert Brooke, 1916

Webster's horrors [...] are not, as with his lesser contemporaries, mere theatrical devices to awake a pleasing shudder. They are symbolic incarnations of that spiritual terror and diabolical delight in suffering, which are, to him, central features of the human drama.   David Cecil, 1949

Life, as it appears to Webster, is a moral chaos.   Travis Bogard, 1955

The play is a dramatic symbol of moral confusion, the impossibility of distinguishing appearance from reality in a world in which evil wears always the mask of virtue and virtue the mask of evil.   Irving Ribner, 1962

The tragedy is disjointed and seems to have been written in episodes, not as a whole.   Roma Gill, 1966

In scene after scene Webster presents Vittoria first as the whitest of white devils and then goes on to reveal her inner blackness. In the last scene he gives us the climax of this movement in a virtual fusion of white and black in the parallel of Vittoria and Zanche in death.   Peter B. Murray, 1969

Crafty and hypocritical, the revengers are more repulsive than the wrongdoers they punish. Francisco selects his instruments from the Cardinal's 'black book' of criminals. Compiled by intelligencers for the purposes of blackmail rather than justice, it is the only book one sees in that ecclesiastical dignitary's hands. Even the boy Giovanni [...] is a questionable figure.   J. W. Lever, 1971

Images of animals and disease figure very largely in all three of [Webster's] plays. [...] One finds many references to devils and to witches; and [...] to 'great men', 'princes', 'politic', and 'policy'. [...] All of these images and words are subsumed in a single theme, that of evil. [...] His plays are saturated with a consciousness of human evil.   Ralph Berry, 1972

The White Devil uses laughter and the vocabulary of comedy to [...] depict a breakdown in experience which allows suffering to produce a comic response and comic action to lead to tragedy. Tragedy and comedy are not at odds: there seems little effective difference between them, since both spring from violence and pain, and the most tragic moments are on the whole also the most comic.
                                      Jacqueline Pearson, 1980

The circumstances which Flamineo struggles against were just as familiar in the first decade of the seventeenth century. He bears some resemblance to the so-called 'alienated intellectuals of early Stuart England' [...]. It was frustration rather than exploitation which characterised these men; leaving university they encountered a society unable to use their talents or fulfil their sense of duty, self-esteem and honour. [...] [Flamineo's] situation is more desperate: he suffers from frustration and exploitation ...   Jonathan Dollimore, 1984

The deliberate mixing of forms imparts to *The White Devil* a disorienting sense of fragmentation and uncertainty, a feeling that experience is puzzlingly discontinuous, its perspectives wrenched and shifting, its values unstable and self-cancelling. Webster can therefore present the love between Bracciano and Vittoria as both a heroic passion and a sordid coupling of an ambitious 'strumpet' with her lustful victim.

Charles R. Forker, 1986

Vittoria is not on stage for much of the time and so her literal absences and often mute stage presences provide interesting and telling holes in the play. [...] The import of Vittoria's [dream] speech [I.2.230–56] is conveyed by a series of commentaries, interpretations and interplays. Flamineo's commentary is followed by Bracciano's [I.2.257–69], which is soon followed by Cornelia's censure of it. [...] The dramatic exposition of Vittoria's character completely undercuts any notion of tragic individualism. Her characterisation never develops through soliloquy, nor even through lengthy speeches.

Dympna Callaghan, 1989

The women of *The White Devil* who usurp masculine rhetoric are positioned not only to gain access to male privilege, but also to offer a savage critique of that privilege. Isabella's repetition of Bracciano's vow, for example, apparently intended to salvage his reputation, actually exaggerates and caricatures his pose [...]. Her performance of Bracciano's machismo foregrounds its inherent theatricality.

Christina Luckyj, 1999

Selected glossary of literary terms

Note: terms are defined here in their literary sense; they often have other meanings in other contexts. Cross-references to other glossary entries are printed in bold.

allegory   a literary form in which the characters and events in the story represent something in a **symbolic** way and offer a moral lesson. Allegories often feature characters who are **personified** abstractions, such as Holy Church (William Langland, *Piers Plowman*) or the giant Despair (John Bunyan, *The Pilgrim's Progress*). See also **fable**.

alliteration   the repetition of initial consonant sounds in words placed comparatively near to each other. This can be emphatic or can enhance the effect of **onomatopoeia**. e.g. '*Your tears I'll turn to triumphs*' (IV.1.25).

allusion   a passing reference to something — an event, person, myth, literary work, piece of music — which the writer does not explain, presumably expecting it to be within the reader's general knowledge, e.g. 'will you be an ass, / Despite your Aristotle …' (I.2.68–69).

ambiguous	having two or more possible interpretations, but leaving it in doubt which is correct. Textual ambiguity may be deliberate or accidental.
ambivalent	having contradictory feelings or attitudes towards something; having either or both of two contrary or parallel values, qualities or meanings.
antithesis	a balancing of words or phrases of opposite meaning, e.g. 'my *life* hath done service to *other men*, / My *death* shall serve *mine own* turn' (V.6.50–51).
archaic	words and expressions no longer in everyday use; old-fashioned.
aside	a remark spoken by a character in a play which is unheard by some or all of the other characters on stage. It may be shared directly with the audience.
assonance	identical vowel sounds in words placed comparatively near to each other in a piece of writing to create particular effects of emphasis, echo, **onomatopoeia** etc., duchess/husband/rusty/rough (I.2.238–40).
blank verse	unrhymed **iambic pentameter**.
caesura	a mid-line break in a **verse** line, coinciding with the end of a grammatical unit, e.g. 'You are to fight. Who is your opposite?' (V.2.2)
caricature	an exaggerated, unrealistic character in fiction or drama, built around a limited number of character traits such as greed or naïvety. Such characters often have names like Young Fashion (Vanbrugh's *The Relapse*) or Truewit (Jonson's *Epicene*).
characterisation	the techniques by which a writer creates fictional or **dramatic** characters. These might include description, **dialogue**, **symbolism**, authorial comment, interior monologue, **soliloquy** etc.
climax	a moment of intensity and power to which a play or story has been leading.
colloquial	the language of speech rather than writing, informal in grammar and vocabulary, possibly using dialect or employing the phraseology of slang.

comedy	a **dramatic genre** in which events reach a positive outcome, often concluding in betrothal or marriage, or in the exposure of vice and folly. Although comedy often contains elements of humour, this is not necessarily a prerequisite of the genre.
critical ideology	the particular political or cultural preconceptions and methodology of any given branch of literary criticism. A brief survey of twentieth/twenty-first century critical movements is offered on pages 90–92.
denouement	the unfolding of the final stages of a dramatic or fictional **plot**, usually at or just after the final **climax**.
dialogue	the direct speech of characters in fiction or drama engaged in conversation.
diction	a writer's choice of words. Diction may be formal, **colloquial**, poetic, **ironic**, artificial etc. It helps to create the **tone** and mood of a piece of writing, and in drama can be an instrument of **characterisation**.
double entendre	a word or phrase open to two interpretations, one of them usually humorously suggestive or indecent, e.g. 'I have almost wrought her to it, — I find her coming' (I.2.164–65).
dramatic	pertaining to the **genre** of drama. If you are asked to consider whether part of a play is 'dramatic', you are not being asked to say whether it is *exciting*, but whether it contributes to the overall impact of the play.
dramatic irony	a discrepancy between the perceptions of the audience and those of the characters in a play: *we* know something *they* don't. Dramatic irony may create humour or tension.
dumbshow	a **dramatic** interlude in which a key part of the story is presented without **dialogue**, using mime, action and gesture, often accompanied by music.
eclectic	drawing on a wide range of reference from diverse sources.
emotive language	language that arouses an emotional response in the reader or hearer. Words can have a positive or negative emotive effect (warmth, tenderness; fear, blood); many words are essentially neutral (table, often).

end-stopped line a line of **verse** where the grammatical sense is completed at the end of the line, e.g. 'Be thou the cause of all ensuing harm' (I.2.308).

enjamb[e]ment running the sense from one line of **verse** over to the next without a pause at the end of the line, e.g. 'Methought I saw / Count Lodowick there' (II.2.31–32).

exposition the delivery of crucial information to the audience, usually at the start of a play, filling in the background to the characters and **plot**.

fable an **allegory** in which the characters are animals. In George Orwell's *Animal Farm*, the animal characters represent historical figures from the Russian Revolution and the rise of the Soviet Union. Flamineo's tale of the crocodile (IV.2.224–44) is a fable.

farce a variety of dramatic **comedy** in which the humour derives mostly from complicated situations such as misunderstanding, deception and mistaken identity.

feminine ending a light or unstressed syllable at the end of a line of **verse**, e.g. 'Let me into your bosom, happy lady' (I.2.206).

genre a classification of literary texts (or other artistic forms) according to type. *The White Devil* might be classified as **tragedy** or, more specifically, **revenge tragedy**. Genre classification can be unhelpful in simplifying complex works into convenient terminology. *The White Devil*, for example, also contains elements of grotesque **comedy**.

hyperbole exaggeration, usually for poetic or **dramatic** effect, e.g. 'I'll cut her into atomies / And let th'irregular north-wind sweep her up / And blow her int' his nostrils' (IV.2.42–44).

iambic pentameter a line of **verse** consisting of five iambic feet (see **metrical foot**).

imagery a pattern of related images that helps to build up mood and atmosphere, deepen our response to character or develop the **themes** of a literary work.

irony a discrepancy between the actual and implied meaning of language, illustrated in its crudest verbal form by sarcasm, for example when Vittoria talks of the 'manly blow' given her by her killers (V.6.232).

machiavel	a devious, scheming politician, based on an English misreading of the Italian political philosopher Niccolo Machiavelli; a common **stereotype** of Jacobean drama, embodied in *The White Devil* primarily by Monticelso and Francisco.
malcontent	someone with a grudge against society, who adopts an air of bitterness and melancholy; a common **stereotype** of Jacobean drama, of which Flamineo is a typical example.
masque	a form of entertainment combining elaborate poetry, music and scenic spectacle, particularly popular at the courts of James I and Charles I. Dramatists of the period often introduced masque-like elements into their plays, such as the barriers scene at the start of V.3 of *The White Devil*.
metaphor	an imaginative identification between one thing and another, e.g. 'How long have I beheld the devil in crystal?' (IV.2.88).
metatheatrical	a self-conscious awareness in a play of its status as a theatrical performance. Such an awareness might work through the persistent use of theatrical **metaphor**, or through more substantial devices such as a play within the play.
metre	a particular pattern of rhythmical organisation based on the number and distribution of **stressed** syllables in a line. There are a number of common metres in English **verse**, the most common being **iambic pentameter**.
metrical foot	one unit of a line of **verse**, consisting of two or three syllables with different patterns of **stress**. For example, an **iambic** foot has two syllables, the second of which is stressed. The **metre** is determined by the number of particular kinds of feet in a line.
morality play	religious drama popular in fifteenth- and sixteenth-century England, often in the form of **allegory**, peopled by **personified** abstractions such as Knowledge, and representative characters such as Everyman.
narrative	story-telling.
onomatopoeia	the use of words that imitate the sounds they describe (e.g. fizz, spit, crash, 'pashed' (I.1.12); or a combination of words where the sound seems to echo the sense (e.g. 'murmuring of innumerable bees' [Tennyson, *The Princess*], 'the stuttering rifles' rapid rattle' [Wilfred Owen, 'Anthem for Doomed

Youth']). **Assonance** and **alliteration** can often be used to create an onomatopoeic effect.

oxymoron
a condensed **antithesis**; usually a phrase of two words, apparently opposite in meaning, which ought to cancel each other out, e.g. 'darkness visible' (John Milton, *Paradise Lost*); 'oppressive liberty' (George Eliot, *Middlemarch*) 'unsociably sociable' (III.3.76); 'unfortunate revels' (V.3.8).

personification
a variety of **metaphor** which attributes human qualities to something inanimate or abstract, e.g. 'thy sins /Do run before thee to fetch fire from hell' (V.6.139–40).

plot
the organisation and structuring of the **narrative** and its characters in a novel or play.

prologue
a speech that precedes the main action of a play, often spoken by a character not involved in the story.

prompt-book
the annotated copy of a playscript used in managing and running a theatrical performance.

proscenium
'picture-frame' stage that creates a clear visual demarcation between the play and the audience.

prose
the language of everyday speech and writing, distinguished from poetry or **verse**.

pun
a play on words, sometimes for humorous effect. It commonly plays on two words of similar sound but different meaning, e.g. travail/travel (III.2.6) or a single word containing more than one meaning, e.g. 'piles' (III.3.9).

quarto
small-format early printed book (10 x 8 inches), usually containing the equivalent of a single play. *The White Devil* was first published in a 1612 quarto edition.

resolution
the sorting out of the **plot** and tying up of loose ends at the end of a fictional or **dramatic narrative**, during or immediately after the **denouement**.

revenge tragedy
a popular dramatic **genre** of the late sixteenth and early seventeenth century, with a central character motivated by vengeance, against individuals or society in general.

rhetoric
the art of using language to persuade. Rhetoric was taught as a subject in Elizabethan schools, modelled on classical examples, identifying a whole range of specific linguistic techniques which

a good persuasive speaker or writer was expected to use. Many of the words explained in this glossary are rhetorical terms.

rhyme identical sounds repeated at the ends of **verse** lines in a variety of patterns. The last stressed vowel sound and everything that follows it should be identical, e.g. fame/name, checks/necks (V.5.10–15).

rhyming couplet a pair of adjacent **rhyming** lines.

satire a literary form in which people, institutions and aspects of human behaviour are attacked through humour, by being made to appear ridiculous.

semantic field a pattern of words associated with a particular topic or aspect of experience. Webster uses **imagery** derived from a wide range of semantic fields in *The White Devil*.

sententia a brief moral or proverbial observation. *Sententiae* are a regular feature of Webster's **dramatic** style, and are often presented in the form of **rhyming couplets**.

simile an imaginative comparison of one thing with another, drawing attention to itself by using the words *like* or *as*, e.g. 'Thou has led me, like an heathen sacrifice …' (IV.2.89).

soliloquy a speech in a play, usually of some length, delivered by a character alone on stage. The character may address the audience directly, or we may feel we are sharing their thoughts. Traditionally, soliloquies were considered to reveal the genuine feelings of a character, free of equivocation and deception.

sources the inspirations, drawn from history, mythology or other literary and **dramatic** works, that writers build into their own artistic vision.

stereotype a fictional or **dramatic** character conforming to a narrow set of characteristics assumed to be typical of a particular group.

stress the natural emphasis we put on particular syllables in words when we speak. Used to construct rhythmical patterns of **metre** when composing **verse**.

subplot a subordinate storyline in a fictional or **dramatic narrative**, with its own set of characters, that works alongside or interlocks with the main **plot**.

subtext   the meaning implied by or underlying the explicit language of a text.

symbolism   the explicit or implied representation of a thing or idea by something else. A dove may symbolise peace, or a heart, love. Literary and dramatic symbolism may be subtle and complex.

tableau   the visual arrangement of characters and objects as if in a picture.

tetrameter   a line of **verse** consisting of four **metrical feet**.

theme   an issue or idea developed in a work of literature. Most complex texts have a variety of themes.

tone   a particular quality in the use of language that may indicate the writer's or speaker's attitude to the reader or listener, or may create a particular mood or atmosphere. A tone may be formal, sincere, pompous, gloomy, **ironic**, solemn, cheerful etc.

tragedy   a **dramatic genre** focusing on the downfall or death of one or two central characters, usually of elevated social status.

tragicomedy   a dramatic **genre** mingling elements of **tragedy** and **comedy** and normally arriving at a happy ending. The contrasting elements may be in separate sections or interwoven throughout the play.

trochee   a **metrical foot** consisting of two syllables, with the **stress** on the first.

unities   'rules' of drama, originally propounded by Aristotle in the fourth century BC, that the action of a play should consist of one unified **plot**, enacted in one location and taking place within a single day. Called the unities of time, place and action, these were disregarded by most Jacobean dramatists, including Webster.

verse   language organised according to its rhythmical qualities into regular patterns of **metre**. Verse may or may not **rhyme**, but is usually set out in lines.

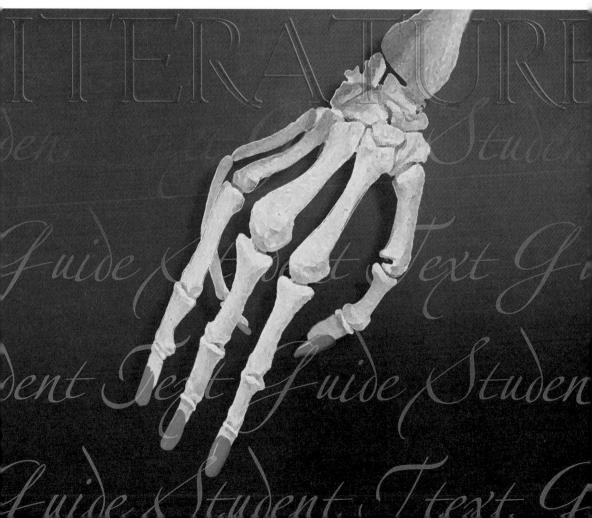

Questions & Answers

Essay questions, specimen plans and notes

Coursework essays

In choosing a coursework essay, you must always check with your teacher that it fits the requirements of the course you are following. For example, it would be foolish to choose a title that focuses on Assessment Objectives that are not covered in the coursework part of your specification.

You may have valid ideas of your own for an essay title or subject. Again, these should be discussed with your teacher. Make sure you know the number of words allowed for the essay.

For coursework specifications that allow a creative response to the text, the exam boards provide guidance and ideas that you should read carefully before deciding on your approach.

Suggested titles

1 What kind of a play is *The White Devil*? How successfully do you think it works as a text for the theatre?

Here are some ideas for tackling this essay:

- discussion of revenge tragedy in the context of Elizabethan and Jacobean theatre
- staging requirements of outdoor theatre for which it was first performed
- exploiting contemporary taste for sensational and violent subject matter
- analysis of structure of play including balance of serious and comic scenes/characters
- the use of dumbshows and ghosts
- consideration of the play's length and whether cuts are needed to tighten its dramatic structure
- the play's portrayal of its society, and the effect of setting it in Italy
- effectiveness of the play's characterisation and the scope for actors to create an impact, both individually and in relationships with others
- examination of some key scenes and their effectiveness
- the play's language and its variety — verse and prose, colloquial, poetic, use of *sententiae*
- effect on the audience, e.g. how moving, tragic impact, comic elements, arousing inappropriate laughter etc.
- consideration of successful productions

2 How is the world of the play created through language, visual effects and music? What kinds of stage setting, costume and lighting might enhance the play's impact in a production?

3 What is your response to the character of Vittoria? How does she develop during the play, and do you think it is valid to regard her as the 'White Devil' of the title?

4 Explore the character of Flamineo, showing how he develops through the play and saying how convincing you found him.

5 Choose any two characters who offer interesting points for comparison and contrast. Write an essay comparing their characters and roles in the play, saying what you thought of them. (Suggestions: Francisco and Monticelso; Camillo and Isabella; Marcello and Lodovico; Cornelia and Zanche; Bracciano and Giovanni.)

6 Explore the relationship of *either* Vittoria and Bracciano *or* Vittoria and Flamineo throughout the play.

7 How does Webster present the women in the play? Examine the characterisation and role of the female characters.

8 Does Webster succeed in individualising the minor characters so as to make them interesting parts to act as well as contributing to the dramatic effects of the play? Consider six or seven examples to support your answer. (Suggestions: Antonelli, Gasparo, Hortensio, Julio, the Conjurer, the Lawyer, the ambassadors.)

9 Write about the different kinds of humour and comedy in the play. How do you respond to humour in the context of a tragedy? Do you think Webster is always in control of where an audience might laugh?

10 Write about some of the themes you consider to be important in the play and show how they are developed.

11 Write about the imagery of the play and the effects it creates.

12 How appropriate is it to classify *The White Devil* as a Gothic drama?

13 Choose one scene, or a self-contained segment within a scene, and give a full analysis of it, commenting on what it reveals of characters and themes; its dramatic effect; its supporting imagery; and anything else that interests you.

14 Choose one scene and describe how you would present it on stage. (You will need to give some preliminary account of the type of theatre you envisage as well as the overall production style.)

15 Examine the structure of the play, looking at how Webster arranges the scenes to create an effective dramatic development, to build up tension and to vary the mood of the play. Consider the way particular scenes are structured, as well as the impact of the play's climax and the effectiveness of its ending.

16 What issues are raised by the title of the play?

17 Imagine you are a director who wishes to mount a production of *The White Devil*. Explain in a preliminary note what kind of theatre and company you work for (large or small; amateur or professional; rich or poor; commercial or subsidised; indoor or open-air; traditional or experimental; touring or home-based), then write a letter to your Artistic Director or Board outlining your reasons for considering this a good play to stage, and giving an outline of your approach to the production.

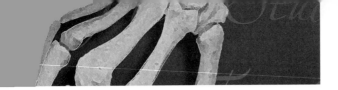

18 Write a review of any production of the play — on stage, film or television — that you have seen. You should comment on the interpretation of the play and the characters; the sets, costumes, music, lighting, performances; and anything else you consider important. If you are lucky enough to have seen more than one production, you could write a comparison.

19 How useful have you found it to study the play in the context of Webster and his time?

20 How has your understanding of the play been enhanced by your reading of a variety of literary criticism? What critical views have you encountered that you consider particularly interesting, revealing or controversial?

21 Write a comparison of *The White Devil*, or any appropriate aspect of it, with another Jacobean play that you know well. (*The Duchess of Malfi*, *The Revenger's Tragedy*, *The Changeling*, *'Tis Pity She's a Whore*, *Hamlet*, *Othello* or *Antony and Cleopatra* would be good choices.)

22 Write a comparison of *The White Devil*, or any appropriate aspect of it, with any other text(s) of your choice, e.g.

■ Ghosts and the supernatural in *The White Devil* and Emily Brontë's *Wuthering Heights*, or Toni Morrison's *Beloved*.

■ Political corruption in *The White Devil* and David Hare's *The Absence of War*.

■ Murder and retribution in *The White Devil* and a modern murder mystery by Agatha Christie, Ruth Rendell, P. D. James etc.

■ Powerful women portrayed in *The White Devil* and *Antony* and *Cleopatra*, or *The House of Mirth* by Edith Wharton.

■ Racial attitudes in *The White Devil* and *Othello*, or *To Kill a Mockingbird* by Harper Lee.

Tackling production-related questions

Responding to a production

There can be no substitute for seeing a play in performance — preferably on stage. There is an electricity about live performance, a sense of danger and risk as well as of shared experience, that cannot be captured on film or television.

The White Devil is an effective performance piece, but you should be prepared for disappointments. It is an extremely difficult play to bring off successfully, partly because of its mixing of genres and its shifts of tone, and partly because of its excessive violence.

Your response to a production will be as personal and subjective as that to any other cultural experience. You should, however, make some attempt to understand what it was trying to achieve, and judge it accordingly.

The impact of a production may depend on the kind of theatre in which it is staged. A small, intimate theatre, with the audience on three or four sides, can offer a kind of psychologically intense and detailed performance that may be more difficult to achieve in a large theatre with a proscenium stage. A large theatre, though, has more scope for spectacular presentation.

- Clues to a production's approach and emphasis will often be found in publicity materials such as brochures and posters, and in the programme. These are always worth looking at, both before and after you have seen the show. What signals do they give about the play itself and the approach taken to it in the production?
- Theatres today rarely have stage curtains which are closed before the performance. What clues were there to the production style in what you saw as you took your place in the theatre before the play started?
- The opening moments of a production will also signal its style. How did the production begin? Was there music, or a visual display or dumbshow, or the swift creation of a stage setting, or anything else not specified in the text?
- What was the point of such an opening, and how effective was it?

When reflecting on a production, there are various aspects to consider.

The world of the play

- What was the overall setting of the play? Was it performed in the period in which the story is set, or the period in which the play was written, or in a modern setting, or some other period? Perhaps there was a more eclectic approach, with elements from a variety of periods and cultures?
- Why do you think this decision had been made? Did it work? In particular, if a modern setting was chosen did you find it helped you to understand the social and political aspects of the play, or was it jarring to see the characters using guns and mobile phones while speaking of daggers, letters and Greek mythology?
- Had any attempt been made to create a different setting and atmosphere for the play's different locations, e.g. Camillo and Vittoria's house in Rome, the courtroom, Bracciano's palace in Padua?
- Was much scenery or furniture used? Was there any use of backdrops or projections? What kind of colour-schemes were employed? How were lighting, music and sound effects used to enhance the mood and atmosphere of the settings?
- How strongly was Italian society portrayed as prejudiced in its attitude to the non-white characters, Zanche and Mulinassar? Was the cast of the production racially varied? How did this affect the audience's response to the characters and attitudes?
- How were the characters costumed? Did their costumes suggest appropriate ideas about their personality, social status and dramatic role? What costume changes did characters have?

- Were there any particularly striking effects? How were key moments staged — the dumbshows, the trial scene, the papal election, the barriers, the ghost scenes, the death scenes?

The use of the text
- Were you aware of any cuts, alterations, additions or transpositions? Why do you think such textual changes were made?
- Were any characters doubled? Was this merely expediency, or did it make a particular point?
- Where did any intervals come in the play? Were they at appropriate moments or did they break the dramatic continuity?
- Was the text well spoken? Was the story told clearly? Was any special emphasis given to particular words, lines or speeches?
- Was the performance effectively paced?

The performances
In responding to actors' performances, it is particularly important to recognise the difference between a bad performance and a performance that differs from your own understanding of a role. A bad performance might be technically inadequate — inaudible, lacking in energy and charisma, delivering lines without apparently understanding their meaning etc. An interpretation of a role may be misguided or perverse but brilliantly performed, and should cause you to reassess your own assumptions about the character.
- Which performances were most powerful and effective? What made them so?
- Which performances created most comedy? Was this effective and appropriate?
- Were you surprised by any of the actors' interpretations?
- Did any roles come to life in performance in a way that they didn't when you were just studying the text?
- Did you like any of the characters, or were they played unsympathetically? Did you feel that the performances were true to the spirit of the play?
- Did the actors work well together as an ensemble?

Your overall response
- Did the production work well for you as a theatrical entertainment? Were you engrossed, amused, excited, moved or bored? How can you explain these responses?
- Did the production do justice to the play? Did it change your view of the play?

Tackling comparative questions

In any comparative essay, you need to keep clear in your mind what the focus of the comparison is. There will always be something in the focus element that links the different texts you are comparing:

- a *theme* such as revenge or madness
- a *character type*, such as malcontent, machiavel or tragic hero
- a *cultural issue* such as the role of women or attitudes to race
- a *dramatic technique* such as the use of dumbshow or soliloquy
- a *linguistic feature* such as the use of blank verse or metaphorical language
- a *plot device* such as ghostly appearances, violent death

The interesting element of a comparative essay is more likely to be the *differences* rather than the *similarities* between the texts you are comparing. In many cases, the best approach is to run through the similarities and connections in your opening paragraphs, leaving most of your essay to explore differences and contrasts between the texts.

Do not tackle a comparative essay by writing an analysis of Text 1 followed by an analysis of Text 2, with a brief summing up at the end. This is not a comparison, but two mini-analyses. Instead, you should be comparing a particular aspect of the topic across both texts in every section of your essay. Useful words and phrases to help you to move from one text to the other and back again include *in contrast, on the other hand, conversely, however, whereas.*

Comparing more than two texts is particularly complex, but again it is important to engage in the act of comparison throughout the whole essay.

For further ideas about planning and writing comparative essays, look at Essay plan 2 (pages 115–17).

Exam essays

You can use the questions below as the basis of your own exam practice: to refine your brainstorming and planning skills, or to tackle a complete essay in the appropriate time limit. Make sure you choose the type of question that is relevant for the specification you are following. Remember to refer to the *play* and the *audience*, not the *book* and the *reader*. Remain imaginatively aware of the play's *performance* potential.

Whole-text questions

Genre and context

1 How useful is it to consider *The White Devil* as a revenge tragedy?
2 How might the play's original audiences have responded to its portrayal of the church, in the character of Monticelso and the staging of the papal election?
3 How far does the play offer a critique of Jacobean England, and how does Webster make his audience aware of this?
4 How are Renaissance attitudes to women *or* racial difference *or* madness reflected in the play?

5 What is your understanding of tragedy, and how far do you think *The White Devil* conforms to traditional expectations of tragic drama?

6 How differently do you think modern audiences would respond to the play, compared with audiences of Webster's time? Which particular aspects of the play might arouse the most divergent reactions?

Characters

7 Whom do you consider to be the play's central character? Justify your choice.

8 How do you respond to the character of Vittoria? Do you find her admirable or despicable?

9 Compare and contrast the characters of Bracciano and Francisco.

10 To what extent do you think Webster intends Isabella and Cornelia to be examples of moral virtue?

11 What is Zanche's role in the play and how do you respond to her?

12 Show how Monticelso operates in *two* scenes from the play.

13 Examine how Webster creates Flamineo's multi-faceted personality, and comment on what the role offers to an actor.

14 Write about the dramatic impact of any *two* scenes in which Lodovico plays a key role.

15 Write about how Webster portrays *either* husbands and wives *or* mothers and sons in the play.

16 How successful is Camillo as a comic character, and how do you respond to his death?

17 Choose five or six of the minor characters and assess their function in the play.

18 How does Webster balance realism in his characterisation with the portrayal of stereotypes such as the malcontent and the machiavel?

Setting and atmosphere

19 What features of the play do you think help to produce its Gothic atmosphere?

20 Analyse how Webster creates atmosphere in *two* of the following scenes: Bracciano and Vittoria's first encounter (Act I scene 2), Vittoria's trial (Act III scene 2), the papal election (Act IV scene 3), Bracciano's madness and death (Act V scene 3).

21 Compare and contrast the atmosphere created in the two ghost scenes.

22 How does Webster evoke the atmosphere of impending disaster in the final scene of the play?

23 How would you create the atmosphere of any *one* scene of the play in a modern stage production? Consider the use of set, costumes, lighting, music, movement and sound effects, and explain how these would support specific features of the text.

Themes

24 What view does the play take of religion?

25 In portraying female subjection *and/or* racial difference, do you think Webster is simply demonstrating the preconceptions of his time, or does he have any moral points to make about these issues?

26 How does Webster portray *either* love *or* lust in the play?

27 The play is partly a revenge tragedy. What does it have to say about revenge?

28 How important is the issue of social status in the play?

29 Characters in the play persistently deceive others through lying, disguise and false appearances. What overall view does the play seem to take of this issue?

30 How far are we shown examples of moral virtue in the play, and what status do they have in the overall impression it creates?

Structure and dramatic effect

31 Many critics have complained that *The White Devil* is clumsily structured. How far do you agree?

32 What place do *either* the dumbshows *or* the ghosts have in the play's dramatic effect?

33 How effectively does Webster switch between the comic and the serious, particularly in the early part of the play?

34 Where might an audience laugh in the play's final scene, and how appropriate is such a response?

35 What strikes you as *either* clumsy *or* dramatically effective in the relationship between Zanche and Mulinassar that develops in Act V?

36 Choose *one* scene of the play that you consider represents a powerful dramatic climax, and examine how Webster achieves this effect.

Language

37 What are some of the recurring images that Webster uses in the play, and what effect does such imagery have?

38 Why and to what effect does Webster employ moral *sententiae* in the play?

39 How and why does Webster vary between prose and verse in *The White Devil*?

40 Argue *for* or *against* the view that Webster is a great poet but not a great dramatist.

Contrasting critical viewpoints

41 In 1856, Charles Kingsley found Vittoria typical of 'all bold bad women'. In 1987, however, Dena Goldberg assessed her as 'the victim of a marriage arranged by her family'. How do you respond to these opposing views?

42 The editor of the Revels Student Edition, John Russell Brown, considers that the play lacks 'any identifiable theme or argument beyond the notion that sin is bad and is usually paid for'. Irving Ribner, however, calls the play 'a dramatic symbol of moral confusion'. Which of these views seems most defensible to you?

43 Writing about the play in 1818, 'H. M.' remarked on its 'disjointed' structure — an adjective used also by Roma Gill in 1966, who added that the play 'seems to

have been written in episodes, not as a whole'. This Student Text Guide, in contrast, argues that the play has a series of carefully interlocking structures (see pages 79–80). Write an assessment of these contradictory views and offer your own response to the play's structure.

44 In 1893, William Archer claimed that Webster has 'no conceivable purpose except just to make our flesh creep', relishing violence for its own sake, while in 1989 Margaret Loftus Ranald noted 'Webster's detachment and ironic worldview'. Which of these views do you take of the play, or can you offer an alternative analysis of its tone and purpose?

45 In Philip Prowse's 1991 National Theatre production of the play, Vittoria and her family were all played by black actors. Reviewing the production, Christopher Edwards commented, 'why this racial element was introduced is a little puzzling', while Lyn Gardner thought the 'exciting casting of black actors as Vittoria's family fits the play like a glove'. What do you think the point of such casting might have been, and how appropriate do you consider it in terms of the play itself?

Comparative essays

46 For centuries, Shakespeare's plays have been regarded as far superior to those of his contemporaries. Write a comparison of *The White Devil* with a Shakespearean tragedy of your choice, arguing for the artistic/dramatic superiority of *either* Webster *or* Shakespeare.

Questions 47–51 would be suitable for AQA B Unit 3.

47 Write a comparison of the treatment of ghosts and the supernatural in *The White Devil*, *Macbeth* and *Wuthering Heights*.

48 Write about the themes of power and/or ambition in *The White Devil* and two texts out *of Macbeth, Dr Faustus, Paradise Lost Books 1* and *2, Frankenstein* and *The Pardoner's Tale*.

49 Explore the similarities and differences in Webster's portrayal of love and passion in *The White Devil* and that of Emily Brontë in *Wuthering Heights* and Bram Stoker in *Dracula*.

50 Write about the elements of *The White Devil* and *The Bloody Chamber* that might justify regarding them both as Gothic texts. What features do they share, and what makes them different?

51 How are devils presented in the action and imagery of *The White Devil*, *Dr Faustus* and *Paradise Lost Books 1 and 2*?

Questions 52–56 would be suitable for OCR Unit 3.

52 Are women presented with a feminist or anti-feminist slant in *The White Devil* and *either The Wife of Bath's Prologue and Tale* or *Paradise Lost Book 9*?

53 How do Webster in *The White Devil* and *either* Chaucer in *The Wife of Bath's Prologue* or Milton in *Paradise Lost Book 9* create characters through the language in which they speak?

54 How do Webster in *The White Devil* and *either* Chaucer in *The Wife of Bath's Prologue and Tale* or Milton in *Paradise Lost Book 9* or Marvell in 'To his Coy Mistress' *or* Blake in 'The Sick Rose' deal with love and lust?

55 How are the themes of power and oppression dealt with in *The White Devil* and in 'The Tyger' and some of the other *Songs of Innocence and Experience*?

56 Webster frequently uses *sententiae* to express moral, intellectual and philosophical ideas. How does *either* Blake *or* Marvell achieve similar effects in the poems you have studied?

Passage-based questions

When tackling passage-based analysis, depending on the precise nature of the question, you should consider the points outlined below:

- Is the section in prose, verse or a mixture of the two? What is notable about the way these language modes are used?
- What is its place in the development of the plot?
- What is going on between the characters present, and what is the impact of any entrances and exits?
- What is the impact of characters who say little in the section?
- How does the language of the scene reveal character?
- What is the balance between dialogue and soliloquy, longer and shorter speeches?
- How does the section support the wider imagery and themes of the play?
- How is the stage picture, together with action and movement, suggested through the dialogue and any stage directions?
- Are there any levels of irony or dramatic irony in the sequence?
- Which characters engage the audience's sympathy, and why?
- What is the function of the set section in the dramatic structure of the play? Are there any parallels or contrasts with other episodes? What would the play lose without this section?

1 Reread Act I scene 1. How far do you find this scene appropriate and effective as the opening of the play?

2 Examine Flamineo's character and motivation as revealed in Act I scene 2 lines 309–55.

3 Look again at Act II scene 1 lines 144–278. How do you explain Isabella's behaviour in this sequence, and how do you respond to her character?

4 Reread Act II scene 2. What impression does Webster create of the Conjurer in this scene?

5 Write a detailed analysis of Monticelso's account of a typical whore (III.2.78–101).

6 Look at the opening of Act IV scene 1, as far as Monticelso's exit at line 76. How does Webster throw light on the devious strategies of politics and politicians in this section?

7 Read again Act IV scene 2 lines 72–128. How does Webster manipulate our view of Vittoria here?

8 Look again at the first half of Act IV scene 3, the papal election, as far as Monticelso's exit at line 70. What do you find dramatically effective about this scene?

9 Compare the way in which Webster presents the madness of Bracciano (V.3.82–130) and Cornelia (V.4.66–113).

10 What similarities and differences are there between Webster's presentation of Isabella's ghost (IV.1.98–118) and Bracciano's ghost (V.4.117–52)?

11 Reread the conclusion of Act V scene 3 (from Zanche's entry at line 216 to the end of the scene). How integral is the intrigue between Zanche and Mulinassar to the plot of the play?

12 Compare Flamineo's fake death speeches (V.6.93–145) with his real ones (V.6.234–76). What effect do you think Webster is trying to create here?

13 Reread the very end of the play, from the English ambassador's line at V.6.277. How might this conclusion be staged and performed to create different impressions of Giovanni's character and authority?

Essay plans

1 How are mothers *and* fathers presented in the play?

Possible ideas to include in a plan

Introduction

- The play has two mothers (Cornelia and Isabella) and one father (Bracciano) as characters.
- There is also the 'absent' father of Flamineo and his siblings.
- Between them, these characters present contrasting models of parental love and responsibility — partly reflecting attitudes prevalent at the time.

Mothers

- Cornelia offers most rounded portrait of a mother.
- Her favourite child, Marcello, seems to share her moral values, but she condemns the behaviour of Flamineo and Vittoria.
- She makes many statements about the pain of being a mother, e.g. 'the curse of children' (I.2.281–83).
- Maternal feelings are complex: she is prepared to curse Vittoria (I.2.299–301) but refrains from stabbing Flamineo after he has killed Marcello — she does not want to lose both sons.
- Grief for her dead son drives her mad.

- In contrast, Isabella is not portrayed in the play's action as a mother, but as a wronged wife. She does not talk to or of her son.
- It is only through Giovanni's grief for her death that her maternal love is stressed: unlike other aristocratic mothers she breastfed her son in person, which he interprets as a sign of her love.

Fathers

- Bracciano's onstage relationship with his son seems cold: he says far less to him than the boy's uncle Francisco.
- He allows his son to be used as a bargaining chip in his political machinations — his expressions of love for his son are politically motivated.
- He responds to Giovanni's distress at his poisoning by asking for the boy to be removed (V.3.15–16) and does not refer to him again.
- Flamineo's resentment at his social position is directed via his mother at his father's irresponsibility in squandering the family fortune (I.2.318–20).

Conclusion

- Views of parenthood in the play are not exactly positive.
- Mothers, however loving, are presented as unhappy, even tragic figures.
- Fathers are distant, remote, irresponsible.
- Thus the play presents what we might these days call dysfunctional families.

Top band marking guidelines

Note: not all AOs are relevant to all essays.

AO1 Coherent and lucid expression in a well-organised and relevant answer. Confident handling of concepts in accurately written style. Sharply focused on task.

AO2 Close focus on how language of text presents views of parenthood. Able to assess role of mothers/fathers in narrative/thematic structures of play. Aware of importance/significance of an 'absent' character.

AO3 Not applicable.

AO4 Contextualises negative views of parenthood as appropriate to tragic genre and supportive of play's social criticism. Aware of importance of cultural context: views of parenthood different in 17th/21st century.

2 Compare Webster's treatment of ghosts and the supernatural in *The White Devil* with Shakespeare's in *Macbeth*. (NB Do *not* write about Shakespeare's portrayal of witches and witchcraft or Webster's use of the Conjurer.)

Possible ideas to include in a plan

Introduction

- Two ghosts in *White Devil*, one ghost and a floating dagger in *Macbeth*.
- Some obvious similarities in presentation, but also more striking differences.

Similarities and differences

- Isabella's ghost, Bracciano's ghost and Macbeth's dagger appear when only one character is on stage, but Banquo's ghost appears in a group scene even though only Macbeth sees it.
- All three ghosts are silent (could contrast with, e.g. the ghost of Hamlet's father).
- Thus, audience may interpret ghosts and dagger as hallucinations — signs of characters' psychological instability.
- Ghostly appearances have different impact on characters: dagger urges Macbeth to murder; Banquo's and Bracciano's ghosts provoke feelings of guilt and terror; but Isabella's ghost, supposedly conjured by Francisco to motivate his revenge, is dismissed by him as irrelevant.
- Ghostly appearances *do* different things: dagger moves, points, vanishes, reappears with blood on it; Banquo's ghost sits, stands, moves, disappears, reappears, pursues Macbeth; Bracciano's ghost moves in on Flamineo, throws earth, shows skull etc.; but Isabella's ghost does nothing.
- Ghost etc. in *Macbeth* form part of a web of imagery derived from semantic field of supernatural; this is less prevalent in *White Devil*.

Staging the supernatural

- Almost certain that ghosts were represented by actors on stages of Globe and Red Bull.
- But what about dagger — could it have been suspended on wires?
- Modern productions make different decisions: possible for Isabella's/Banquo's ghosts not to appear on stage, but more difficult with Bracciano's ghost because of business with skull/earth/flowers etc.
- How do these decisions affect audience interpretation of characters/world of play? If ghosts are not seen on stage, this puts emphasis on psychological interpretation of characters and plays down the actual possibility of an evil, supernatural world influencing them.
- How do modern attitudes to ghosts etc. affect modern stagings/audience response?

Conclusion

- Briefly sum up key points made.
- Note that these two plays not necessarily representative of how ghosts etc. were portrayed in other plays of period.

Top band marking guidelines

Note: not all AOs are relevant to all essays.

AO1 Coherent and lucid expression in a well-organised and relevant answer. Accurate written style handling concepts with confidence. Close and detailed knowledge of both texts. Sharply focused on task with confident comparative structure.

AO2   Close focus on how language and dramatic structure of texts shape meaning and audience response. Able to place supernatural elements within wider structure of plays.

AO3   Able to range confidently across both texts making comparisons and drawing on a wide range of supportive examples and references. Equally confident on both texts.

AO4   Aware of both texts as products of same cultural/theatrical context. Confident placing of supernatural elements within contemporary beliefs, ideas and dramatic conventions. Aware of staging issues in assessing dramatic impact and how modern attitudes can alter/manipulate audience response.

Sample essays

The two essays that follow are not offered as realistic examples of what an AS/A-level candidate could actually hope to write in an exam, but to give a sense of how different types of question might be tackled.

The first essay offers an assessment of the character of Giovanni, and the second examines the key theme of policy in the play. In real examination circumstances, without the text available, such essays could still be produced, but with a more limited range of quoted material, and without the act, scene and line references.

The same questions could have been tackled in a variety of different ways, with considerable change of focus and emphasis from different candidates. Your own knowledge and understanding of the play and its contexts should give you the confidence to write effective essays on any subject the examiners can devise.

Sample essay 1

How far does Webster portray a growing maturity in Giovanni's character as the drama unfolds?

The young prince, Giovanni, makes seven appearances in *The White Devil*, four of which place him at the centre of attention. When we first see him, in Act II scene 1, he seems almost stereotypically childish and naïve, with an interest in playing at soldiers and a precocious wit. At the end of the play, he administers justice like a morally authoritative adult, commanding obedience and being granted the play's closing words. On the face of it, then, it does seem that Webster presents a 'growing maturity' in his character.

In his first words (II.1.6–7), Giovanni's military interests are established as he reminds his uncle, Francisco, that he had promised to him 'a horse / And armour'. When he reappears later in the scene he pursues the theme, demanding 'a pike' (II.1.109) and going on to give an account of the behaviour he would exhibit in leading an army. He envisages himself as a heroic leader, the 'foremost man' at the head of his 'troops', charging the 'French foe' (II.1.122–23) — in contrast to those generals who make a great deal of noise without putting themselves in danger (lines 116–19). He seems here to be a typical boy, playing at war, but as he prattles on he shows another side to his character in his sexually

knowing jokes about the inevitable attractions of men towards women. As Monticelso aptly remarks, he is a 'Witty prince' (II.1.136).

His childish naïvety is well illustrated by the way he is employed here by the adults as an innocent pawn in their awkward attempts to negotiate an improvement in their personal and political relationships. Monticelso is condescending in his attitude to him, pointing out to Bracciano his son's virtuous qualities and the future hopes that are embodied in him. In urging Bracciano to set Giovanni a moral example through his own behaviour, and to be a 'pattern' to him (II.1.105) he is implicitly — and, it appears, successfully — using the boy as a bargaining chip, exerting a kind of moral blackmail. Nothing could better demonstrate the child's impotence and lack of awareness.

Giovanni is present in the dumbshow enacting his mother's poisoning, at which his 'sorrow [is] expressed', and when we next see him he is in mourning for her. His childishness is again to the fore in his touching grief combined with his ignorance of what it actually means to be dead. He tries to avoid telling Francisco directly of Isabella's death, knowing it to be something that will make him sad, and he tries to imagine an after-life in which the dead 'eat, / Hear music, go a-hunting, and [are] merry' (III.2.324–26) — a kind of home-from-home. He reveals that he has not slept for six nights and is pleased to hear that death is a kind of sleep, since it means his mother will no longer suffer the grief that has kept her sleepless and weeping for nights on end. This again emphasises his childishness, for he seems to show no understanding of why his mother might have been so unhappy; the adults, of course, as well as the audience, are aware that it was because of Bracciano's unfaithfulness. Particularly touching are Giovanni's reflection on how much his mother loved him (III.2.337–39) — on the grounds that, unlike most aristocratic mothers of the time, she apparently breast-fed him as a baby; and his horror at her body having been enclosed in a leaden coffin and his being denied a last kiss (III.2.335–36). Subsequently, he is not spared further tragedy, since he is present at the barriers at which his father is poisoned, expressing horrified shock — 'O my most lovèd father!' (V.3.15) — and then remaining silent for 26 lines, presumably overcome by grief and confusion at the horrific spectacle of Bracciano's suffering and imminent death.

It is a very different Giovanni who appears at the start of the next scene — a difference prepared for by Flamineo's sarcastic and disrespectful comments about him. He is not taken in by his step-uncle's hypocritical flattery, and clearly objects to being cheered up with the argument that, now his father is dead, he is in power. He offers Flamineo a powerful moral rebuke: 'Study your prayers, sir, and be penitent' (V.4.21), following it up with a rather obscure but strongly phrased admonition, given extra authority by its rhyming-couplet form (V.4.22–23). Craftily, Webster opens up for the audience the possibility that the young prince will take on some of Francisco's devious machiavellianism as Flamineo observes, 'He hath his uncle's villainous look already' (V.4.30). Although we are unlikely to trust Flamineo's biased and cynical judgement, we do not necessarily dismiss his observation out of hand.

The newly grown-up Giovanni is shown at his most impressive in the final scene. Although the ambassadors and guards try to keep him back, he comes forward — as he earlier said he would do at the head of an army — and asserts a strong moral and judicial authority. Not afraid to insult the murderers as 'bloody villains' (V.6.283), he demands that they justify their actions. He is indifferent to the fact that the murders have supposedly been committed on his behalf and horrified at his uncle's part in them. The sentences of 'prison' and 'torture' spring easily to his lips, along with an appeal to 'justice' and 'heaven'. He even advises the 'honoured lord' (V.6.298) — presumably the English ambassador — to use the punishment of Lodovico and the others as a moral example, before rounding off the play with a powerful assertion, in another impressive rhyming couplet, that evil deeds rest on a fragile basis — perhaps intended to be the play's moral lesson too. There is nothing remotely childish about Giovanni's language in this scene. All his lines could be spoken convincingly by an adult figure of authority.

It appears, then, that in his last two scenes, Giovanni has changed from innocent child to mature young man. However, to say that Webster shows his '*growing* maturity' is misleading, since the playwright makes no attempt to portray his development as a *process*. Giovanni simply turns into a different character between V.3 and V.4, and it would be up to an actor to decide how far this change might be demonstrated as happening more gradually. As with any play text, theatrical performance can develop what is only hinted at on the page.

Sample essay 2

What does Webster mean by 'policy', and how are politicians portrayed in *The White Devil*?

'Policy' is one of those words that can be misleading to a modern reader or audience because their meaning has shifted since the early seventeenth century. Today, the word is largely neutral, meaning simply a plan of action pursued by an individual, organisation or government. In Webster's time, however, it had strongly negative connotations, suggestive of scheming, craftiness and manipulation to achieve one's desired ends. The term was closely associated with the ideas of Machiavelli — or rather with a simplistic misinterpretation of his ideas by English readers. In the drama of the time, characters who operate by 'policy' are frequently placed in supposedly corrupt foreign settings, particularly Spain or, as in *The White Devil*, Italy. The stereotype of the machiavel is invariably linked with policy and is represented in Webster's play by a number of characters, notably Francisco and Monticelso.

Confusingly for modern readers, derivatives of the noun 'policy' carry the same associations. Hence, the adjective 'politic' and the noun 'politician' inevitably imply distrust and disapproval. In particular, a politician is not, as in modern usage, someone who is engaged in the process of local or national government, but anyone who operates by devious and underhand means. Thus, while the two characters just mentioned are politicians in both the modern and the seventeenth-century sense, even a socially inferior character like Flamineo might be regarded as a politician on account of the methods he uses.

'Policy' and its derivatives are key words throughout *The White Devil*, and Webster offers frequent generalised comments on its operation and implications. It is a word

frequently on the lips of Flamineo, who first uses it as a general indictment of women's hypocrisy: they hold back their sexual favours, he suggests, not out of modesty but to keep their partners interested in them; in this, he says, 'they are politic' (I.2.21). At the end of the same scene, though, he offers a useful definition of 'policy' that one might keep in mind throughout the play. Comparing his devious intentions to winding rivers and crooked paths that imitate 'The subtle foldings of a winter's snake', he concludes, in a rhyming couplet that highlights it as a thematic statement:

> So who knows policy and her true aspect,
> Shall find her ways winding and indirect. (I.2.354–55)

Flamineo's brother, Marcello, is presented as a virtuous contrast to him, and this contrast is emphasised by his attitude to policy. When both are facing trial on suspicion of being involved in Camillo's death, Marcello advises Flamineo to 'stride over every politic respect' in order to embrace virtue and honesty. This is partly offered as a warning since, while 'politic respect[s]' may bring about advancement or promotion, they also 'infect' those who thrive by such methods (III.1.58–60). Already, Webster is presenting us with alternative viewpoints on this key theme.

As well as the generalities expressed on the subject of policy, however, Webster shows it in action through the characters of the play. Flamineo recognises his sister's implicit use of policy when she recounts her dream to Bracciano:

> Excellent devil!
> She hath taught him in a dream
> To make away his duchess and her husband.
>
> (I.2.257–59)

Her policy is evident on other occasions too, as when she feigns acquiescence to Flamineo's suggested suicide pact in order to turn the tables on him. Only once, though, is the term applied specifically to Vittoria — unfairly, as it happens — when she denies knowledge of Francisco's love letter in what Bracciano styles her 'politic ignorance' (IV.2.81). Flamineo, too, employs policy to achieve his ends, explicitly embracing it in his definition of the term already quoted, and in assuming his disguise as a 'politic madman' (III.2.309). On one occasion the term is used, ironically, of the hapless Camillo who, 'by his apparel', Flamineo remarks, might be 'judge[d] a politician'. As so often in this play, though, appearances are deceptive, and Camillo is merely 'an ass' (I.2.48–51).

Camillo is, in fact, the victim of 'policy' rather than its practitioner. His death is contrived by Bracciano and Flamineo through the 'politic strain' (II.1.316) of the vaulting-horse — praised by the Conjurer as a 'far more politic fate' (II.2.35) than that of Isabella's murder by means of her husband's poisoned picture. Bracciano's operation of such murderous 'policy' is what motivates the revenge plot against him, as Lodovico gloatingly emphasises when Bracciano is at the point of death. He mocks

Bracciano as 'You that were held the famous politician; / Whose art was poison' (V.3.155−56) and relishes the working of the poison he himself has administered to Bracciano, 'A-melting in your politic brains' (V.3.164).

The play's key politicians, however, are Monticelso and Francisco — 'that old dog-fox, that politician Florence' as Bracciano calls him (V.3.94). Their machiavellian methods are evident in every scene in which they appear, presenting the audience with a variety of lessons in the subtleties of 'policy' and its practical application. They are first seen working together in Act II scene 1, manipulating Bracciano towards a feigned reconciliation, in a kind of classic good cop/bad cop routine that craftily alternates Francisco's passion with Monticelso's calm reasonableness. Bracciano is not fooled by this, deliberately drawing Francisco in — 'Now you that are his second, what say you?' (II.1.45) — and provoking him to anger. All three of them are guilty of cynically manipulating the young prince, Giovanni, as a 'champion [who] / Shall end the difference' between the brothers-in-law (II.1.95−96). The fragility of such a peace is evident in Flamineo's later observation of the 'whispering' between Francisco and Monticelso and their 'invisible cunning' (II.1.283−88) — a phrase aptly descriptive of the workings of 'policy'.

Policy and teamwork rarely go together, however, and apparent cooperation is almost invariably a tool to achieve the ends of the individual. Though Francisco and Monticelso never exactly fall out, their aims diverge. Act IV scene 1 is like a cat-and-mouse game between them, in which Monticelso advocates policy rather than open violence, on the grounds that 'undermining more prevails /Than doth the cannon' (IV.1.13−14), while Francisco apparently rejects, in his 'innocence', the achieving of his ends by 'treacherous acts' (IV.1.22). The Cardinal's 'black book' (IV.1.33) is a classic instrument of policy, but there is no explicit discussion of how Francisco might use the names it contains. At the end of the scene he reveals his hypocrisy by admitting, when alone, that he shares Monticelso's belief in policy, noting that 'He that deals all by strength, his wit is shallow' (IV.1.131). One of the play's unanswered questions is whether Monticelso's outraged condemnation of Lodovico as the instrument of Francisco's revenge (IV.3.117−27) marks a change in his moral outlook following his election as Pope, since he does not appear again in the play. No such moral transformation operates in Francisco, however, who immediately tricks Lodovico, with a bribe of a thousand ducats supposedly from Monticelso, into believing that the new Pope's attack on him was merely for show, masking his underlying 'cunning' (IV.3.149).

Webster's constant reiteration of the term 'policy' and its variants marks it as more than just a recurring image, promoting it instead as a central theme of the play. It will be clear from the examples discussed that it is not something Webster invites us to view with approval, however much we might sometimes admire the craftiness and wit that its practitioners demonstrate.

Further study

Editions of the play

All good editions of *The White Devil* contain useful notes and stimulating introductions. Some of the best are listed below.

Brennan, E. M. (ed.) (1966) New Mermaids, Ernest Benn.

Brown, J. R. (ed.) (1966) Revels Plays (2nd edn), Methuen.

Brown, J. R. (ed.) (1996) Revels Student Editions, Manchester University Press. This is the edition that has been used for the textual references in this Student Text Guide.

Hart, C. (ed.) (1970) Fountainwell Drama Texts, Oliver & Boyd.

Luckyj, C. (ed.) (1996) New Mermaids (2nd edn), A. & C. Black.

Mulryne, J. R. (ed.) (1970) Regents Renaissance Drama series, Edward Arnold.

Trott, A. (ed.) (1966) Macmillan's English Classics, Macmillan.

Weis, R. (ed.) (1996) in *'The Duchess of Malfi' and Other Plays*, World's Classics, Oxford University Press.

Criticism of Webster's plays

Aughterson, K. (2001) *Webster: The Tragedies*, Palgrave.

Berry, R. (1972) *The Art of John Webster*, Clarendon Press.

Bradbrook, M. C. (1980) *John Webster: Citizen and Dramatist*, Weidenfeld and Nicolson.

Cave, R. A. (1988) *'The White Devil' and 'The Duchess of Malfi': Text and Performance*, Macmillan.

Esche, E. J. (ed.) (2000) *Shakespeare and his Contemporaries in Performance*, Ashgate. This contains a stimulating essay by Nick Tippler, 'Cunning with Pistols: Observations on Gale Edwards's 1996–7 RSC Production of John Webster's *The White Devil*'.

Gunby, D. C. (1971) *Webster: 'The White Devil'*, Studies in English Literature 45, Edward Arnold.

Holdsworth, R. V. (1975) Webster: *'The White Devil' and 'The Duchess of Malfi': A Casebook*, Macmillan.

Moore, D. D. (1981) *Webster: The Critical Heritage*, Routledge & Kegan Paul.

Pearson, J. (1980) *Tragedy and Tragicomedy in the Plays of John Webster*, Manchester University Press.

Ranald, M. L. (1989) *John Webster*, Twayne.

Criticism of Jacobean tragedy

Brooke, N. (1979) *Horrid Laughter in Jacobean Tragedy*, Barnes and Noble.

Callaghan, D. (1989) *Women and Gender in Renaissance Tragedy*, Harvester Wheatsheaf.

Dollimore, J. (2004) *Radical Tragedy* (3rd edn), Palgrave.

Ellis-Fermor, U. (1958) *The Jacobean Drama*, Methuen.

Gibson, R. (2000) *Shakespearean and Jacobean Tragedy*, Cambridge Contexts in Literature, Cambridge University Press.

Hopkins, L. (2002) *The Female Hero in English Renaissance Tragedy*, Palgrave.

Simkin, S. (ed.) (2001) *Revenge Tragedy*, New Casebooks series, Palgrave. This includes a stimulating essay by Christina Luckyj, 'Gender, Rhetoric, and Performance in *The White Devil*'.

Context

Braunmuller, A. R., and Hattaway, M. (eds) (1990) *The Cambridge Companion to English Renaissance Drama*, Cambridge University Press.

Briggs, J. (1997) *This Stage-Play World: Texts and Contexts, 1580–1625* (2nd edn), Oxford University Press.

Gurr, A. (1992) *The Shakespearean Stage 1574–642* (3rd edn), Cambridge University Press.

Gurr, A, (1996) *Playgoing in Shakespeare's London* (2nd edn), Cambridge University Press.

Pritchard, R. E. (1998) *Shakespeare's England: Life in Elizabethan and Jacobean Times*, Sutton Publishing.

Wells, S, (2006) *Shakespeare and Co.*, Allen Lane.

Wiggins, M. (2000) *Shakespeare and the Drama of his Time*, Oxford University Press.

Audiovisual resources and the internet

There have been no major film or television versions of *The White Devil* in recent years, and no audio production is currently available. Searching for the play on the internet offers some rewards, such as details of the 2000 Sydney Theatre Company production, directed by Gale Edwards (who also directed the 1996 RSC production), with Hugo Weaving as Bracciano. The most reliable site is probably the following, though it may prove limited in what it has to offer to AS or A-level students:

www.luminarium.org/sevenlit/webster/index.html

A number of Shakespeare websites contain material on Shakespeare's contemporaries, and theatre websites are likely to have details of current or previous productions of the play. The following may be useful:

- **www.rsc.org.uk** is the Royal Shakespeare Company's website.
- **www.shakespeares-globe.org** is the official website of the reconstructed Globe Theatre.
- **www.shakespeare.org.uk** is the website for the Shakespeare Birthplace Trust. From there you can access the Shakespeare Centre Library in Stratford-upon-

Avon. This houses the archives of the Royal Shakespeare Company, where you can look up the records of its 1996 production of *The White Devil*, including promptbooks, programmes, photographs and reviews. Individual students and small groups can arrange to watch the archive video of the production. Although recorded in performance with a fixed camera, this is nevertheless well worth seeing. Find out more on the website, via the 'Library and Archives' link.

- **www.nationaltheatre.org.uk** is the National Theatre's website, through which you can find out how to access records of its 1969 and 1991 productions of the play. Enter 'archive' in the 'Search' box or go directly to **www.national-theatre.org.uk/archive**